My Fab Fasting Philosophy

To my children, without whom this book
would never have been.

Souls live on through recipes.

Eat well. Live well.

Helen Klaedes

www.myfoodphilosophy.com

Icon Key

SERVES
This icon tells you how many people the dish serves.

PREPARATION TIME
This icon tells you the preparation time required for the dish.

m = Minutes • **h** = Hours

COOKING TIME
This icon tells you the cooking time required for the dish.

m = Minutes • **h** = Hours

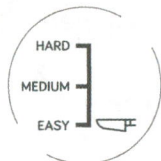

COOKING DIFFICULTY
This icon tells you the level of difficulty each dish is to make.

DISH TYPE
This icon tells you what type/size of dish it is, for example:

M = Main • **S** = Side • **D** = Dessert • **S/M** = Side or Main

VEGAN
This icon means the dish is suitable for vegans and vegetarians.

VEGETARIAN
This icon means the dish is suitable for vegetarians.

Contents

My Fab Fasting Philosophy

We, Greeks, are renowned for our hospitality and for our cuisine. It is well known that our attitude to food and our Mediterranean diet is up there among the healthiest in the world. One of those Mediterranean islands is Cyprus, and, due to its location, its cuisine has strong Turkish and Middle Eastern influences and subtle imprints of European cooking, even though, intrinsically, Cypriot food is Greek.

During the many periods of fasting for spiritual, religious and health reasons, it dawned on me that I have many recipes that I cook often that are essentially vegan or vegetarian. These recipes have been perfected by Greek home cooks for 100s of years and are more relevant today than ever before. This is not a trendy faddy cookbook; it is an up-to-the-minute guide of updated and simplified Greek recipes which have been a mainstay of mine for decades. You will be able to easily recreate in your own kitchen.

The beauty of this cookbook is that you will have, at your fingertips, tried and tested recipes, cooking tips, and details of how to prepare ingredients and which are best to use. I have also included a selection of translations and keywords for ingredients and names of dishes. You will be able to reference this cookbook and prepare a meal from scratch in very little time and with little or no experience and soon make meals by heart.

My children, who have now grown up, all have great cooking skills, but I realised they do not have my recipes for their favourite meals. So, what began as me jotting down recipes for them, developed into a book of my life's personal food journey and memories. You will discover, as you interact with this book, that It is impossible for me to disconnect my personal feelings with food and the tangible anamnesis it evokes. This is, therefore, a food diary as well as a recipe book. As I am a third-generation Greek Cypriot living in the UK and born to Cypriot parents, this recipe book reflects that mixed heritage, part Greek part British, and we describe ourselves as Gringlish or Greeklish, which influences our language, culture and every aspect of our lives.

For us Greeks, food is a philosophy. We live to eat well and experience food and, because of that, we cook with passion and to enhance our lives. You, too, with the help of this informative book, will easily adopt the skills of preparing food that you will connect with and enjoy. By encompassing the mindset required for you to prepare meals with love and generosity, you will taste your food as you cook, smell your ingredients, add only those you like and cook using all your senses.

By using the tips in this book to guide your approach, you can prepare vegetables and salads with the same amount of enthusiasm as if using fish or meat. By infusing them with as much flavour as possible, you will never have complaints again about bland salad and vegetables, and even your fussy eaters will enjoy a larger variety of tastes.

My aim is to provide a guide that helps enlighten those who wish to expand their culinary horizons and remind their taste buds of past holidays in the Greek islands. At the same time, I want to dispel the myth that Greek/Mediterranean food is meat heavy, time consuming, difficult to prepare, and impossible to source the ingredients. I wish to share my knowledge of food and ingredients that will enable you to prepare quick, rustic and nutritious meals with ingredients you can easily find and, yet, will provide you with authentic results. I have included many traditional and customary recipes - albeit adapted somewhat. Many of my special recipes evolved organically due to the constraints of time, ingredients, familial preferences and dietary requirements, but I have tried and tested them all repeatedly over many years. All the recipes included have passed the test of time and have been called upon in quick succession during my daily routine. The key is to choose the right recipe for the right time and to nail the technique for rice, pasta or legumes, which will provide you with the starting point, from which to build greeklicious and balanced meals in no time at all.

Whether you are a practising vegan, vegetarian, flexitarian, or simply want to cut down on your meat or dairy consumption, then this is the book for you. It is packed full of recipes from tasty starters, meals, meze, salads, soups, snacks, dips and desserts, including everything from cooking, shopping and storage tips through to translations, uses for your favourite ingredients and details of how to prepare and use any unfamiliar products, as well as which dishes complement one another. These are wrapped up with their etymology, fables, anecdotes customs and myths. Some of the tales are as legendary, wonderful and memorable as the recipes themselves. Whatever you choose to prepare, it will be Greeklicious and, as we say, "Kali Orexi, Kopiasete" to My Fab Fasting Philosophy.

Helen Klaedes

Understand your ingredients

 A basic knowledge of key ingredients is essential in the preparation of food. The following chapter is a quick and simplistic appraisal of key ingredients referred to in my recipes, which once you are familiar with, should dispel any uncertainty or fears you may have of certain products or unfamiliar ingredients.

Oil   Λάδι

I believe, as most Greeks do, that olive oil is one of the most essential ingredients in culinary terms. Not only does it provide us with a fabulous flavour, it is also packed with anti-oxidants, has anti-inflammatory properties, and helps stave off illness. Olive oil is also antibacterial and generations of Greek parents in my family have massaged their babies skin from birth with olive oil, I believe it introduces the skin to external factors, and builds up the immune system in a beneficial way. The Ancient Greeks discovered the restorative and healing properties of olive oil, as well as its culinary benefits. It was also used for medicinal purposes. So, it's worth re-examining the way you think of olive oil as it is an exceptional gift from Mother Nature, which is rich in mono-unsaturated fats, that we should enjoy daily.

When choosing which oil to use, follow this guide:

When the recipes states extra virgin olive oil, use an olive oil that says extra virgin olive oil, and which is dark green in colour. This oil is not to be used in cooking or frying, as it does not heat to a high temperature and the taste changes when heated. Olive oil is light sensitive. If possible, store in a dark bottle and a cool dark place.

Light in colour, olive oil and light olive oil are a composition of refined olive oils and extra virgin oil.
This type of oil can be used for cooking but not frying.

The following few examples of oils can be used for baking, cooking, frying and roasting, as they heat to a high temperature and have a neutral flavour; vegetable, sunflower, rapeseed, grapeseed and groundnut.

You can also use a mixture of light in colour olive oil and a neutral cooking oil if you like. I often do this, as I like the health properties and taste of light olive oil in food, but require the combination of both as the neutral cooking oils have the ability to heat to higher temperature.

Greek Cheeses   Τυριά

Halloumi Cheese   Χαλούμι

There are fresh and aged varieties of halloumi cheese. They are produced in exactly the same way although the length of time the cheese is initially kept in brine determines the texture of the cheese.

Fresh halloumi is the one widely available in shops, and is soft, creamy and slightly rubbery. This is great for grilling, frying and baking. There is also a lower fat alternative to fresh halloumi.

Aged halloumi is the one that Cypriot homes usually buy from specialist shops or bring back in their suitcases from a visit to Cyprus. Aged halloumi cheese has a firmer texture, which lends itself to being grated and can be used to stir into pasta, cakes and bechamel sauce. Cypriots call grated cheese 'Trimmah' - 'Τρίμμα' and, translated simply, means grated or tiny crumbs. Aged grated cheeses are also used as a seasoning - much like parmesan. As aged halloumi may be difficult to find, there are many good alternatives, such as 'Graviera, kefalograviera' (not to be confused with Swiss Gruyere) or 'kefalotyri' (very salty - use one third less of this than recipe states if substituting for halloumi), dry anari, parmesan, or freeze fresh halloumi. Grate straight from the freezer.

Anari   Αναρι

Anari or curds are a by product yielded from the production of halloumi and can be fresh or dried. Fresh anari is highly perishable and is hard to find, as it mostly originates from the small artisanal/cottage industries which produce home-made halloumi, and is very similar to ricotta. Cypriot anari has been the winner of the prestigious silver medal award won at 'The World Cheese Awards'.

Cypriot dry anari is easier to find, as it is lasts longer and can be packaged. It is, however, best used for grating, as it is quite hard.

Feta Cheese   Φέτα

This is a crumbly cheese which is creamy in texture and a little salty. The word 'feta' means 'slice' as, once formed, the block of cheese is sliced. It is very easy to find in many shops. Check the label for where it is made, as there are many imitations. Greek feta, however, is unique in flavour, and is a product which The European Union has given 'Protected Designation of Origin 'status.

Olives   Ελιές

Olives are classed as fruit. Unripe olives are green and change purple/black when ripe. Unless using as an ingredient in a recipe, olives are best eaten with pits as they are fuller in flavour.

Haldiki – Χαλκιδική
are pale green olives which are plump and tasty.

Kalamata – Καλαμάτα
Olives are purple/black in colour and can be wrinkled or firm in texture.

Tsakistes – Τσακιστές
or cracked olives are undoubtably the Cypriot favourite. These freshly harvested green olives go through a process of being cracked - thus the word 'Tsakistes'. Traditionally, each olive is cracked using a heavy pebble as a tool, to reveal the olive stone, without breaking the entire fruit. They are then placed in jars of cold water, which needs to be changed twice a day for 15-20 days. If, at this point, they have lost their bitterness, the water will be drained. The olives will then be brined for 24 hours and drained again. The olives are then put into clean jars with lids and marinated and stored in lemon juice, cracked coriander seeds, lemon slices, sliced garlic cloves and a pinch of salt. The storage jars are filled to the brim with extra virgin olive oil. You must try these if you come across them abroad. Cypriot households preserve olives to this day in the same age-old method of generations, and once you taste them, you will understand why they go through such an intensive process.

Potatoes   Πατάτες

Potatoes come in many varieties. Generally speaking, in culinary terms, they fall in to two categories:

Floury Potatoes - these are great all rounders and can be used for mashing, roasting and frying. Great examples are 'The Cypriot Spunta', 'Diamant', 'Cara' and the varieties of potatoes you will be familiar with such as 'King Edward', 'Maris Piper' and Red Rooster.

Waxy Potatoes - these are good for boiling, as in for salads, stews and casserole dishes. These types are also good with the skin left on and roasting. Common varieties of these are 'Charlotte', 'Anya', 'Desiree' or any variety of the small potatoes you find packaged in the supermarket.

Vegetable Stock   Ζωμός Λαχανικών

You can purchase really good quality stock cubes, stock pots or ready-made fresh stocks in the chilled section of the supermarket. Look out for the low sodium/salt varieties. Stock pots are far easier to stir into food when cooking. If you prefer, and have time and wish to do so, you can make your own stock.

To make 2 pints of a basic vegan stock:

- 2 Large carrots. Rinse, discard top and bottom stalks.
- 2 Large celery sticks, preferably with leaves. Rinse before using
- 1 Large onion. Peel
- 2 Bay leaves
- 30g Flat leaf parsley. Rinse before using
- 1 Tsp whole black peppercorns
- 2 Pints water

Roughly chop all the vegetables, Simmer gently for one hour, then pour through a sieve to strain. Will keep refrigerated for up to 3 days or in the freezer for 1 month. The above recipe is a good basic one, but you may add leeks, tomatoes, fennel or parsnips. If you prefer a darker coloured stock, do not peel the onion.

Spice Clove   Γαρίφαλο

Spice clove is a small black flower-bud used as an aromatic spice, Greeks believe that spice cloves have medicinal/painkilling properties. We bite on a whole clove when we have toothache. We also use spice cloves and cassia bark in our tea, along with our favourite tea bag and in many culinary recipes.
Do not confuse with a clove of garlic, which is also used as a flavouring.

Garlic Clove   Σκόρδο

Garlic is classed as a vegetable. One garlic clove is one segment from a whole head of garlic; each segment has a thin paper like skin which needs to be removed before it can be minced or chopped. Garlic cloves are a superfood - highly nutritious, low in calories, reduces blood pressure, combats colds, detoxifies and helps lower cholesterol.

Cinammon   Κανέλλα

Cinnamon is a spice and it is literally grown on trees. It comes ground, in quills or as bark. Cassia/cinnamon bark and quills are harvested from the same tree, but the bark is the thicker outer layer of the tree, whereas cinnamon sticks or quills are the inner secondary husk of the tree. These roll up like parchment paper when peeled off the tree, these have a stronger/medicinal flavour which manufacturers use for ground cinnamon, as it has a far more intense flavour. Cassia bark has the same taste and health properties but is far more mellow. Cinnamon is believed to regulate blood sugars, is an anti oxidant and an anti inflammatory. As you become familiar with my recipes, you will find that I often add cinnammon in some form or other. If you do not like the taste of it simply leave it out. As it is a flavouring, it will not disrupt the ratio of ingredients/recipes, this applies especially in baking where precise measurements are required.

Anise seed   Γλυκάνισο

This is the seed of a flowering plant that grows in the Mediterranean and Asia, it tastes similar to liquorice, fennel or star anise. Although sweeter, it is classed as a spice. In Cyprus it is predominately used to make a herbal medicinal tea, two Tsp of anise seeds per one mug of water; brought to the boil and add honey or sugar to taste. We call it Γλυκάνισο – 'yliganisso'. Not only does it taste exceptional, but is highly regarded to release feel-good endorphins, which is why we drink it when we are ill, or as a digestif. Many modern pharmaceutical companies use anise seeds to make heartburn and indigestion remedies. Anise seeds are used to make the round purple sweets known as aniseed balls, and it is used to flavour the infamous Cypriot alcoholic beverage called Ouzo.

Legumes and Pulses

Φασόλια και Όσπρια

All legumes are edible plants that grow in pods such as green beans, edamame, mange tout and peanuts, which, although the name implies otherwise, they are indeed a legume.

Lentils are a pulse, which are the seeds harvested from a plant, and come in green, black or red varieties. Other examples of pulses are kidney beans, split peas and black-eyed peas, all of which are high in protein, fibre and iron, and are a nutritious substitute for meat.

Chickpeas

Ρεβύδια

They are classed as a pulse that are very high in protein and fibre. Tinned chickpeas are great for homemade hummus, or toss them in light olive oil and roast them along with your favourite spices, to nibble on like nuts. Retain juice from tinned chickpeas, as it is used as a vegan alternative to whipped cream or as a thickener for savoury and sweet recipes alike. This liquid is called 'Aquafaba'. It can also be whipped into stiff peaks, then baked into meringue.

Simple Vegan Chocolate Mousse Recipe

Whisk the aquafaba juice with sugar and a pinch of salt, until it forms stiff peaks (can take up to 10 minutes.)
Melt chocolate in a bain-marie until it melts. Do not heat chocolate.
Add the chocolate into the mousse, fold the two together with a spatula, divide into glasses or bowls, and chill for at least 2 hours before serving. Decorate with a fruit berry of your choice and more grated chocolate.

Rice

Ρύση

Rice is a seed from a grass and is classed as a cereal grain.
Always rinse raw, and drain rice before cooking, To cook raw long grain rice, using the absorption method, is to double the volume of water to rice - 1 cup rice = 2 cups of water. Boil on a low to medium heat until small holes begin to bubble on the surface of the rice. Do not boil rice on too high a heat. It will absorb liquid too quickly and still be chalky in the centre. Stir only once halfway during cooking time. Otherwise you will have sticky rice. Push aside a little of the the rice in the centre of the pan using a fork, near the end of cooking time, if you are not sure if the liquid has been absorbed. Do not let rice boil dry. Switch off heat, put a lid on, and allow it to stand for 10 minutes. The residual heat will make the rice light and fluffy and any excess liquid will be absorbed. Use a fork to fluff the rice before serving.

Orzo Pasta   Κριδαράκι

Orzo is a type of pasta which is indigenous to Greece/Cyprus.
Do not rinse orzo, as it is a type of pasta. Although it is shaped like rice, it should be cooked on a very low, slow heat and stirred constantly. This catches out even the most experienced of cooks. When cooked, the orzo should be completely soft, and the dish should be served fluid, similar to a risotto, and slide off the spoon.

Pasta   Συμαρικα

If you have prepared a pasta sauce to go with your pasta:

1. Cook it in a pan large enough to contain the added finished pasta.
2. You should boil the pasta 2 minutes less than stated on the directions on the packet.
3. Finish cooking the pasta together with the sauce.
4. Retain a cup of the cooking stock to add to the drained pasta and sauce if required.

Chocolate   Σοκολάτα

Chocolate is made from roasting and grinding the seeds farmed from the cacao fruit tree. This process extracts cocoa butter and cocoa solids, which are then flavoured and processed into cocoa powders, chocolate etc.
Dark chocolate above 70%, and dark cooking chocolate are very often suitable for vegans. Check the ingredients list on all dark chocolate bars, as vegan chocolate can be far more expensive and more difficult to source. Milk chocolate is, as the name implies, invariably made with the addition of dairy products. White chocolate, in fact, does not contain any cocoa beans or chocolate whatsoever. It is made wholly from dairy cream and sugar.

Cordial / Squash   Σιρόπι

Cypriots have made cordials for hundreds of years, as it was an early method of preserving crops in the hot climate. Rose, banana, lemon, orange, carob and almond cordials are all time honoured, authentic and exceptionally good cordials. Look for the Greek brands, as they do not normally contain preservatives. The rose and banana flavours are especially good when made up with cold milk for great tasting milkshakes. They are also ideal made up with ice cold water for a refreshing drink, I have also tried replacing dairy milk with chilled almond or coconut milk, which work equally as well. I have used these cordials in a lot of the dessert recipes. The lemon cordial is exceptional, as are all the citrus fruits in Cyprus. This is made up with ice cold water into a long drink that is simply the best lemon squash you will ever taste. Carob syrup - 'Χαρουπομελο' is made from the carob tree native to Cyprus, I recall it is a strange looking tree that has long black beans hanging from its branches. We would stop if we came across one of those trees. We would pull off a bean and squeeze out the dark sweet carob syrup. It was known as black gold, as it was nearly as expensive in weight. It is used like honey, and sweets are made from it. Almond cordial is the original almond milk, an ancient recipe made from almonds, sugar, and rose water. Dating as far back as the Roman Empire, it is made up with hot water as a warming, soothing drink called 'Soumadha' - 'Σουμάδα'. It was the drink of choice offered to guests at engagement, wedding and christening parties. Orgeat syrup is an Italian version of Soumadha, which you might be familiar with. It is used in cocktails such as a Mai Tai.

Afrosa   Αφρόσα

This is a powder and is a Cypriot digestif used since the Ottoman Empire. It is essentially a sweetened sherbet, which you add to a tall glass, pour cold water into it, stir, and down very quickly, as it froths over the rim of the glass. The word 'Afrosa' is derived from the Greek word for foam/cloud which is 'Afros'.

Baking Powder   Μπέικιν πάουντερ

This is a raising agent often used in cake making. This powder is activated when liquid is added to it. Without getting too technical, there are four golden rules to its successful use in baking:

1. Once incorporated into a recipe, you should not let the raw mixture stand for too long, as the active ingredients will lose their effectiveness and you will be left with a finished product that has not risen as it should.
2. Once your cake/dish is in the oven, do not open the oven door too soon, as this will cause your cake to stop rising.
3. Do not underbake your cake, as this will cause it to sink in the middle once cooled.
4. Measure out as per recipe; not enough baking power and your cake will not rise, too much BP your cake will taste bitter, and it will rise too quickly, then collapse.

Σούπες

Soups

Ντοματόσουπα

Greeklicious Tomato soup

Ντοματόσουπα

I have kicked off with this very simple to make, yet harmoniously well balanced soup, as it is my Greek interpretation of a British classic, tweaked a little here and there, with the addition of my personal favourite ingredients, yet still completely recognisable as the family favourite. We all need a bowl of every now and then. Contrary to baking, savoury dishes are forgiving of little variations of your preferred ingredients, so go ahead and opt for the herbs you prefer.

   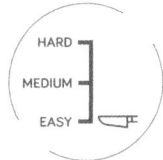  

Preparing the Soup

- 1 ¼ Kg ripe tomatoes (any size, shape variety as long as they are red and very ripe.) Rinse
- 1 Medium onion. Finely chop
- 1 Small leek. Discard outer leaves, trim root and part of the fibrous green leaves, rinse really well, dry, and finely chop
- 1 Carrot. Peel, trim top and bottom stalks. Finely dice
- 1 Large floury potato
- 1 Celery stick. Trim top and bottom, rinse, cut in four lengthwise, then finely chop
- 2 Large cloves garlic. Peel and mince
- 1 Tsp finely-chopped basil, mint or parsley
- 2 Bay leaves
- 3 Tbsp light olive oil
- 2 Tbsp tomato purée
- 2 Tsp dried oregano
- 2 1/2 Pints hot vegetable stock suitable for vegans
- Salt and freshly ground pepper

Cooking Method

1. Preheat fan oven to a high heat. 280-290 degrees C
2. Discard stalks and cores of tomatoes. Place on a large greased baking tray. Lightly season with salt and pepper and roast for 8-10 minutes
3. Add the light olive oil to a large saucepan and heat on a medium heat. Add the onions, celery, carrot, potato, and leeks. Sauté for 5-6 minutes until the onions and leeks are soft and translucent, stirring regularly. Turn down heat if the vegetables are browning and continue to soften
4. Remove tomatoes from the oven and leave them to one side
5. Stir in the garlic, tomato purée and dried herbs and cook out for a minute to release and enhance flavours
6. Add the tomatoes to the pan one at a time removing skins as you do. Pour any juices from baking tray into the pan too, pour in the hot stock, stir well
7. Bring to the boil, add salt and pepper to taste, then turn down heat to a gentle simmer with the lid on for 20-25 minutes. Stir a couple of times
8. Turn off heat. Discard bay leaves
9. In a good processor or a hand blender blend your soup until it is smooth. Taste and adjust the seasoning accordingly. If you want your soup a little redder in colour, stir in another tsp of tomato purée

Serve with crusty bread, crumbled feta or a swirl of plain greek yogurt, cream, or extra virgin olive oil.

> **Top Tip.**
> This soup can be frozen in an airtight container. Reheat thoroughly and check seasoning before serving.

Footnote.
If the soup tastes a little tart for your taste, add a little sugar.

Σούπα με Πράσο

Lush Leek Soup

Σούπα με Πράσο

'Braso' - 'Πράσο' is the Greek word for leeks. It is derived from the word 'Brasino', which is the word for the colour green in Greek. I have made this leek and potato soup many times over the years. It is tried, tested and much loved - another family favourite which I needed to record for posterity. This vegan soup recipe has helped me on many occasions rustle up a quick, nutritious bowl of soup and is especially appreciated when guests come to visit during days of fasting. The leek is the perfect example of a great crossover and regional ingredient that has also been grown for a number of years in the Mediterranean. It is used as the base for this soup resulting in a satisfyingly familiar combination of flavours.

   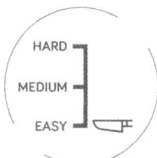  

Preparing the Soup

How to clean leeks.
Trim off the roots and the fibrous, coarse, dark green parts of the leaves and discard them; cut in half lengthwise; separate the leaves down to the centre leaves; immerse in cold water. Use a vegetable brush to scrub clean, as leeks are a muddy vegetable. You may need to change water and rinse them again depending on how dirty they are. Drain. Pat dry.

- 4 Large leeks. Chop the clean leeks into slices
- 2 Large potatoes - floury ones such as Desiree, King Edward, Maris Piper. Peel and cut into large dice
- 1 Large onion. Peel and roughly chop
- 3 Garlic cloves. Peel and mince
- 4 Tbsp light olive oil
- 1 Vegetable stock cube suitable for vegans
- Salt and freshly ground pepper to taste
- 3 ½ Litres of water

Cooking Method

1. Heat the oil in a saucepan on a medium heat, add the onions and sauté for 2-3 minutes until they begin to go translucent

2. Stir in the garlic and follow quickly with leeks, so that the garlic does not burn and become bitter. Sauté for 3-5 minutes stirring occasionally so that the leeks cook evenly

3. Follow with 2 pints of water, in which you have dissolved the stock cubes, then all the remaining ingredients

4. Bring to the boil, then turn down the heat and simmer for 25 minutes or until all the vegetables are soft. Taste and adjust seasonings accordingly

5. Add as much of the remaining water as you please to achieve the consistency of soup you require, and then bring the soup back up to heat. If you add more water, check the seasoning

6. You can use a stick blender or a food processor to blend the soup

Serve with crusty bread.

Footnote.
Skip step 6, where you blend the soup, if you like a chunky texture of soup.

Top Tip.
You can use a waxy potato if you do not mind a more glutinous soup texture.

Αυγολέμονο
Ζούπα

Aphrodites' Avgolemono soup

Αυγολέμονο Ζούπα

This iconic, beloved rice and lemon soup is called 'Avgolemono'. It means avgo-egg, lemono-lemon, which is how this soup is thickened and flavoured. Cypriots and this soup are soul mates. We have songs, parodies and entire sketches dedicated to, if a little tongue in cheek, of our love of this soup. We serve this soup to our loved ones when they are poorly or to mark the end of fasting or lent. We prepare this to greet our relatives when they come home from a long journey and to celebrate births, Christmas and marriages. In fact, we make this as often as possible with little or no reason. This is a vegetarian adaptation of a classic, that I extend heartily. Let's hope the purists take it with a pinch of salt.

   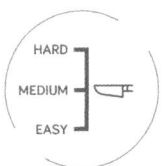  

Preparing the Soup

- 200g Long grain rice. Rinse, leave in a sieve to drain
- 2 Large leeks Discard fibrous outer leaves and the fibrous dark green part of the stalks, separate a few layers until you no longer find mud, dirt. Immerse in cold water and scrub clean. Trim and discard bottom end stalk. Stand the rinsed stalks in a colander to drain
- 1 Large onion. Peel and finely chop
- 2 Small carrots. Discard top and bottom stalks, peel, rinse,and chop into fine dice
- 2 Large eggs. Room temperature
- 2-5 Lemons, juiced with no pips
- 30g Flat leaf parsley. Rins and finely chopped - stalks and all. Keep the stalks to one side
- 1 Tbsp dried mint
- 1 Tbsp dried oregano
- 2 Vegan/Vegetarian stock cubes, dissolved in 3 pints of cold water
- 2 Tbsp light olive oil
- Salt and freshly ground pepper to taste

> **Top Tip.**
> Ensure you follow step 10 as this stabilises the egg in the soup and prevents scrambling. If required reheat the soup gently later.

Footnote.
The lemon ratio stated on the ingredients list may be quite broad but lemons can vary greatly in acidity, as do personal preferences. We Greeks love the taste of lemon and use it liberally.

Cooking Method

1. Finely slice the leeks and leave to one side
2. Heat oil in a large saucepan on a medium heat. Stir in the onions with a wooden spoon for 2-3 minutes until they soften but do not colour
3. Stir in the leeks until they wilt. Turn down heat if your vegetables are taking on colour
4. Stir in the dried herbs, all the chopped vegetables and the chopped stalks of the parsley. Cook for 1-2 minutes
5. Pour in the cold stock and bring to the boil. Turn down heat to low, stir in the rice, season with salt to taste, and gently simmer for 25 minutes. The rice needs to be completely soft and will have absorbed a lot of liquid
6. Crack and beat the eggs with a fork. Take a jug, which you can stand a small sieve over and pour the beaten eggs into the jug. Let the egg drain in to the jug. This step catches the albumen and will give your soup a better finish. Save the dish you beat the eggs in, to one side. Discard the albumen
7. Stir in the parsley leaves, add pepper, taste and adjust the seasoning, if necessary. Add more water/stock if you want a thinner soup or simply require more portions. Take off the heat (do not bring back to boil if you have added more stock)
8. Stir in the lemon juice to taste, keeping in mind that it should taste of lemon. You should add as much of it that your tastebuds can enjoy. Stir the soup well before next step
9. Pour ¼ of the beaten egg into the bowl you whisked the eggs, add a small ladle of the soup to the bowl and stir with a wooden spoon to combine them both. Quickly stir into the soup. Repeat this step 2 more times. Finally add a ladle of soup to the jug with the remaining eggs. Combine the contents then stir quickly into the soup
10. Put soup back on a very low heat and bring to heat gently until it begins to thicken and the colour deepens, stirring continuously. Taste and adjust seasoning if necessary.

Serve with a garnish of dried oregano or mint and a lemon wedge and more freshly ground pepper to taste.

Τραχανά Ζούπα

Traditional Trahana soup

Τραχανά Ζούπα

'Trahana' is a historically-classic Cypriot soup which is so called because the name of the base ingredient for this soup is called 'trahana'. Bulgar wheat or kibbled wheat was traditionally cooked in yoghurt or fermented milk until it absorbed the liquid and became a pliable dough. This dough was then formed into long rope like strips or patties called 'Trahana'. These patties were then placed on a round woven straw tray called a 'Paneri'. A light muslin or mesh covered the trahana whilst it was air dried on the flat roofs of single-story kitchens. Finally, it was stored with lots of fresh garlic in an airtight container in larders until required. This was a popular way of utilising seasonal produce and preserving it in hot countries before the time of refrigeration and freezing. The scorching hot sun would serve the purpose of drying the mix. I would watch my grandmother make 'trahana' as a child towards the end of the long summer holidays. Utilising any surplus milk, she would make halloumi cheese/fresh anari and trahana amongst other things. The milk would be fermented for a couple of weeks in large urns until it became yoghurt. It was then brought to a boil in large bronze cauldrons called a 'kasanee'. The kibbled wheat and lemon juice would be added and the whole thing laboriously stirred until it became an almost dough-like mixture. All this would be performed in the utility room, known as the 'voiithitiko'. Cypriot homes normally had two kitchens, as Greek women are extremely house proud and liked to keep their kitchens clean at all times. Most families kept their internal kitchens as clean as a showroom and the kitchen sink would be used to display their prized home-grown houseplant. Hard to beleive, but true!

Soaking Time Overnight

   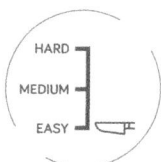  

Preparing the Soup

- 300g Shop-bought trahana, immersed in cold water and soaked for a minimum of 3 hrs
- 1 Vegetable stock cube
- 2 Large lemons, juiced
- 2 ½ Pints cold water
- 1 Tsp dried mint
- Salt and freshly ground pepper to taste
- 100g Cubed halloumi

Cooking Method

1. Add the water and stock cube to a saucepan
2. Using a hand balloon, whisk in the soaked trahana and any liquid in the bowl. Bring to the boil, whisking constantly
3. Turn down heat to a gentle simmer, season with salt to taste, cook the trahana for 15- 20 minutes until it thickens and bubbles and whisk every 2-3 minutes so that it doesn't catch
4. Add the cubed halloumi, pepper and lemon juice to taste. Stir with a wooden spoon, take off heat and serve with lemon wedges

Serve with fresh lemon wedges and freshly ground pepper to taste.

Footnote.
A variation of this recipe is to add 1 whole diced fresh decored tomato and 1 tsp tomato purée at step 1.
If you forget to soak the trahana, simply follow steps 1 and 2. Switch off heat and leave for 2-3 hours. Resume at step 3. Place soup on a very low heat and hand whisk constantly until soup heats through thoroughly. You may also use a hand blender to give the soup a smooth consistency and then go to step 4.

Top Tip.
This soup thickens as it cools, so add more stock if you would like a thinner soup.

Λάχανοσούπα

Voluptuous Vegetable soup

Λάχανοσούπα

Soup is a comfort food wherever you live and Cyprus is no exception. This is greatly similar to minestrone. I'm not sure which came first. Nevertheless, this recipe is delicious. In the long summer months, bowls of traditional 'Auyolemono' and 'Trahana' are consumed in the early hours after an evening out in establishments we call 'Xsenihtika - 'Ξενικτικα', as well as, at home prepared by 'Mamma'. This recipe is associated with providing comfort, as it is customary to take pots of food - especially variations of this soup for those that are recovering from illness or bereavement to nourish and console. Of course, it is also made in times of lent. I love to make this with a variety of fresh seasonal vegetables, although you can make it with as few as you please. Simply keep the orzo which acts as a thickener and the tomato, bay leaf, parsley, and oregano to retain its authenticity.

   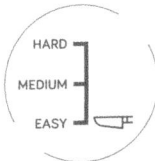  

Preparing the Soup

- 3 Large ripe tomatoes, remove skin, decore and chop into dice, reserving any juices and seeds
- ¼ Cabbage - savoy or sweetheart. Rinse, finely slice, and discard thick ribs
- 3 Celery stalks with leaves. Trim bottom stalks and discard any string by pulling with your finger. Cut each stalk in 4 lengthwise and finely dice
- 2 Large carrots. Peel, rinse, and chop into dice
- 1 Large courgette. Discard top and bottom stalks, rinse, and chop into dice
- 1 Large potato - Cyprus, King Edward, Maris Piper. Peel, rinse, and chop into cubes
- 1 Large onion. Peel and finely chop
- 1 Large garlic clove. Peel and mince
- 100g Orzo pasta or any very small pasta of your choice
- 4 Tbsp light olive oil
- 30g Flat leaf parsley. Rinse and finely chop. Keep stalks to one side as you add them at different stages
- 1 Tsp dried oregano
- 1 Bay leaf
- Salt and freshly ground pepper

Cooking Method

1. 2 1/2 Pints water
2. Heat the oil in a saucepan on a medium heat and sauté the onions for 2-3 minutes until soft but not browning
3. Stir in the garlic, parsley stalks (chopped) and celery, using a wooden spoon. Quickly follow with tomatoes and their juice. Cook for 1-2 minutes
4. Add the water and bay leaf. Stir in the cabbage and courgettes and bring to the boil
5. Turn down heat to a simmer, then add the orzo, potatoes, carrots, and oregano. Stir frequently so that the orzo does not stick to the bottom of the pan. Season with salt and pepper to taste. Cook gently until the orzo and vegetables are soft
6. Stir in the chopped parsley leaves. Cook for 2-3 minutes. Taste and adjust seasoning if necessary
7. Turn off heat and serve

Serve with lemon wedges, crusty bread, or bruschetta scraped with a garlic clove and drizzled with extra virgin olive oil.

Top Tip.
You can swap the orzo with rinsed long grain rice or leave out completely. The addition of one fresh red chilli finely chopped gives this soup a really welcome spice warmth.

Λούβανα
Σούπα

Mellow Yellow Split Pea Soup

Λουβανα Σούπα

Creamy, satisfying and wholesome, a perfectly easy way to prepare a nutritious meal in advance ready for the family coming home. They can dip into before they get to the biscuit barrel. I have found that having a brimming saucepan of food at their fingertips is a great way to entice fussy eaters without further persuasion from the aroma emitted from cooked food ready to be devoured. Soup is a great dish to be reheated in individual portions as required. Split peas are dried, peeled, and processed from the common garden pea. Cypriots refer to these, as well as an edible very bitter flowering plant, as 'louvana' - 'λουβανα'. Although they are related, they are not the same thing. Split peas are packed full of protein.

Soaking Time Overnight

   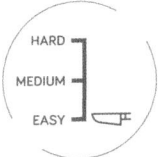  

Preparing the Soup

- 320g Yellow split peas. Soak overnight in cold water (Some yellow split peas do not require soaking. Check the label on the packaging)
- 60g Long grain rice. Rinse and drain
- 2 Onions. Peel and finely chop
- 50ml Light olive oil
- 3-4 Lemons, juiced
- 2 litres vegetable or vegan stock
- Salt and freshly ground pepper to taste

Garnish
- Finely chopped parsley
- Finely diced fresh tomato

Cooking Method

1. Drain the yellow split peas
2. Boil kettle
3. Place peas in a saucepan. Cover with cold water, bring to the boil for at least 10 minutes, when a foam volcano begins to form. Drain the peas, rinse the sides of the pan of any residue and wipe with a clean damp cloth if necessary
4. Add peas back to the pan and cover generously with hot water. Simmer on a medium heat for 20 minutes. If necessary, change the water again before going on to next step
5. Heat a separate saucepan and add the oil, when hot add the onions and sauté until they are golden brown. Take off the heat so they do not burn and become bitter
6. Boil kettle
7. Make up stock
8. Drain peas, add ¾ of the stock and place back on to a medium heat. Stir in the onion, pour the remaining stock into the pan, in which you fried the onion, deglaze, and add to the peas
9. Add the washed rice, season with salt and pepper to taste and continue to simmer for 20 minutes or until the rice and peas are completely soft
10. Stir in the lemon juice to taste, check the seasoning and adjusting if necessary. Take off the heat. Stir in parsley and chopped tomato, if required, when ready to serve

Serve with crusty bread, rocket leaves, radish, black olives.

Footnote.
You can also make a delicious yellow split pea stew instead of soup. Folow steps 1-6.
Reduce stock at step 7 to 600ml, continue with steps 8-10.
Reduce lemon to taste. Simply cook until you have a stew like consistency. Turn off heat and allow to stand for 10 minutes before serving.
Troubleshooting. Not all varieties of yellow split peas require soaking. Check the label on packaging before using.

> **Top Tip.**
> You can use peeled and cubed potatoes instead of rice.

Πλευρές
και
Ελαφρύτερα
πιάτα

Sides & Lighter Dishes

Πουργούρι
Πιλάφι –
Πλιγούρι

Pleasant Wheat Pilaf

Πουργουρι Πιλάφι Πλιγούρι

This dish is made using bulgur wheat, which is parboiled crushed durham wheat used for cooking. It resembles cous cous but cannot be prepared in the same way, as it requires cooking, whereas cous cous simply needs soaking with hot water/stock. Pilaf or pilau simply means a rice or wheat dish cooked in broth. Bulgur wheat has a nutty earthy taste and texture and is available as course or fine ground. Bulgur wheat has been used by the Greeks as far back as the era of ancient Greeks and Romans. The Bible references this staple food stuff. Many Greeks used to refer to this dish as 'poor man's food'. In today's times this is another benefit, as well as the fact that it tastes great and children seem to love it.

   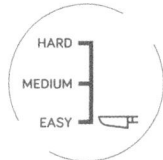  

Preparing the Pilaf

- 320g Course bulgur wheat
- 1 Large onion. Peeled and finely chopped
- 100g Cut vermicelli
- 250g Tomato passata
- 1 Large tomato. Remove skin and core, and dice the flesh and seeds
- 2 vegetable stock cubes, dissolved
- 3 Tbsp of light olive oil
- 640ml Hot water
- Salt and freshly ground pepper to taste

Cooking Method

1. Boil the kettle
2. Place saucepan over medium heat and add oil
3. Add the vermicelli and onion and sauté until both are a really nice bronze colour. Stir a few times and do not allow to burn
4. Stir the bulgur wheat in well to coat the grains in the oil
5. Add the tomato, passata, stock cubes, salt to taste, and lots of freshly ground pepper
6. Turn down heat to lowest possible setting
7. Stir in the water and cook for 10-15 minutes. Stir every couple of minutes. If the pilaf cooks before you are happy with the bite of the grain, add a little more water and cook a little longer
8. Turn off heat and allow pilaf to stand, with a lid on, for 5 minutes before serving

Serve with Greek yoghurt, salad, Mouthwatering Malted Mushrooms or Roasted Mediterranean Vegetables

Footnote.
Cooked bulgur wheat spoils easily. Consume on the same day and refrigerate any leftovers on the same day it is cooked. It will keep for up to two days.

Top Tip.
Break spaghetti into small pieces if you do not have vermicelli.

Μανιτάρια
Ξιδάτα

Mouthwatering Malted Mushrooms

Μανιτάρια Ξυδατα

Cypriots love foraging for free-growing edibles, especially wild mushrooms. They love them so much that the Cypriot Forestry Department has implemented penalties, such as hefty fines or imprisonment, for those that violate the regulations and do not follow the strict guidelines on how to pick them. As Cyprus is situated in the hot Mediterranean and is also a nation of smallholders who grow many varied crops, the Cypriots are experts in preserving ingredients as they have long hot dry summers and mild winters. This dish is a continuation of the method of using vinegar as a preservative. We pickle a variety of ingredients including cauliflower, celery, chillies, carrot, peppers, and mushrooms and if you stop off at one of the many roadside sandwich vans pickles - 'Ξυδατα' are always on the menu.

   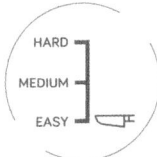 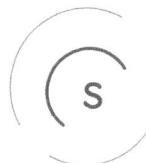 

Preparing the Mushrooms

- 500g Button mushrooms or closed cup or closed cup chestnut mushrooms
- 1 Large cooking onion. Peel and roughly chop
- 3- 4 Tbsp light olive oil or any cooking oil you prefer
- 100ml Red wine vinegar
- 20ml Malt vinegar
- 600ml Water
- Salt to taste

Cooking Method

1. Dunk the mushrooms very quickly in a bowl of cold water and swirl them around to dislodge any dirt/mud Remove and place them in a colander. Do this immediately before you are ready to cook them

2. Cut off the end of the stalks, and if you are not using button mushrooms, cut them in half or quarters so they are roughly the same size. Place them on a kitchen towel as you go along

3. Heat a saucepan on a medium heat, then add the oil. Heat the oil and add the mushrooms and stir. Cook for two to three minutes and turn up the heat to medium high

4. Add the onion and stir. If the pan seems dry, turn down heat. Cook for another minute or two

5. Add the salt, vinegar, and water

6. Turn down heat to low and cook for a further ten minutes or until the liquid has been absorbed and the mushrooms and onion are soft and glossy. If not, add more water and cook a little longer.

7. Turn off heat, put a lid on and allow the mushrooms to marinade

Serve with crusty bread and tabbouleh salad or orzo pasta, rice or a bulgar wheat pilaf.

Footnote.
Can be eaten warm or chilled.

Top Tip.
You can use any white wine or cider vinegar to replace the red wine vinegar.

Κλέφτικο
Νησιώτικο

Not Kleftico

Κλέςτικο Νηστίσιμο

'Kleftico' means 'stolen'. This depicts how Greek guerilla soldiers would survive during the revolution after being miles away from home for days on end; the shepherds would also wander far away from home whilst looking for new pastures for their flocks to graze and, at some point, their paths would cross. My siblings and I actually spent a few summers herding goats. I cannot say I have fond memories of that experience - anyway I digress - back to the guerilla klefthes, who after 'finding' their ingredients, would light a fire deep in the ground and bury them to cook. This method would mask both the smoke and the aromas emitted from the food during cooking. As this variation does not contain meat, it is called 'not kleftico' for obvious reasons. It is cooked low and slow in an oven in a table roasting dish, we call a 'sini', with herbs, onions and tomatoes, making this a superior potato dish.

   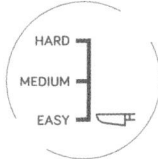  

Preparing the Kleftico

- 1 Kg Cypriot potatoes or waxy potatoes, such as Desiree, Dutch creams or Red Rooster. Peel and rinse. Cut each potato lengthwise into 4 pieces. If potatoes are small, cut them in half again lengthwise
- 4 Large carrots. Peel and discard top and bottom stalks. Rinse and cut each carrot into 2-3 chunks
- 3 Large ripe tomatoes. Discard core, rinse and roughly chop into pieces
- 2 Large onions. Peel and roughly chop into pieces
- 150ml Light olive oil
- 1 Tsp ground cinnamon
- 1 Small stick cassia/cinnamon bark
- 1 Large lemon, juiced
- 2 Bay leaves
- 1 Tsp dried oregano
- 100ml Water
- Salt and freshly ground pepper to taste

Cooking Method

1. Preheat fan oven to moderately hot - 190-200 degrees C
2. Add all the ingredients to the ovenproof dish, except the water and pepper. Mix them all together with clean hands, so that all the ingredients are completely coated with oil and herbs
3. Pour in the water, squeeze in the lemon juice, and grind pepper to taste, over the vegetables
4. Cover with cooking foil, shiny side down
5. Roast in the oven for 45 minutes, and then take off the foil. Turn the potatoes, Place back in the oven without foil and continue to roast until the potatoes take on a little colour and are completely soft. Check the seasoning and serve hot from the oven

Serve with salad and dips of your choice.

> **Top Tip.**
> The onions, tomatoes and juices at the bottom of the ovendish are delicious. Spoon them onto the plate along with the potatoes and mop it all up with crusty bread.

Πατάτες με
Λασμαρι στο
τούρνο

Rosemary Roasties

Πατάτες με Λασμαρι στο Φούρνο

Rosemary grows in abundance in Cyprus, and Greeks believe it to be a sacred plant that is a symbol of love and remembrance. It is used at weddings, christenings, and funerals in floral wreaths, bouquets, and as incense. In Cyprus, we call it 'Lasmaree' - 'Λασμαρι' whereas Greeks from the mainland call it 'Thentrolivano' - 'Δεντρολίβανο'. Rosemary is used sparingly, as it can be quite pungent. It has many uses, such as fragrance for soaps and toiletries. It is used to infuse olive oils, salt, and the woody sprigs can be soaked in water and then used as skewers for kebabs. This recipe is a great introduction to rosemary for those who are not sure of the flavour. After all, who doesn't enjoy roast potatoes?

   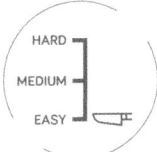 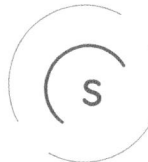 

Preparing the Roasties

- 500g Small baby potatoes. Skin on. Use a variety of potato, such as Anya or Charlotte
- 2-3 Sprigs of fresh rosemary
- 4 Tbsp light olive oil
- ¼ Cup of cold water, roughly 80ml
- 2-3 Garlic cloves. Peel and roughly chop
- Salt and freshly ground pepper

Cooking Method

1. Preheat oven to a high heat, 210-220 degrees C
2. Wash the potatoes and remove any eyes. Leave potatoes whole, but cut any larger ones in half, so that they are all roughly the same size. Drain
3. Put potatoes in a roasting tin. Add the oil and water. Add the whole sprigs of rosemary, as the leaves are inedible unless finely chopped
4. Season with salt and freshly ground pepper
5. Roast in a high oven until the potatoes are golden brown, crispy, and soft in the centre
6. Remove potatoes from oven, spoon into a serving dish and use the rosemary to adorn the dish, or discard if you prefer

Serve with vegetable kebabs, roasted cherry tomatoes, pan fried tender stem broccoli, with garlic and light olive oil.

Top Tip.
Be generous with your portions as these are really moreish.

Λαχανικά
Στο
Φούρνο

Roasted Mediterranean Vegetables

Λαχανικά Στο Φούρνο

This is a mouth-watering good dish; colourful, flavourful, and easily adapted according to the availability and seasonality of the ingredients. Although it is a simple and everyday dish, it always looks and tastes special, and as though you have made an effort. Prepare with confidence. You will enjoy this dish immensely.

  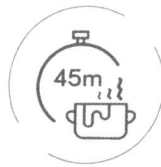 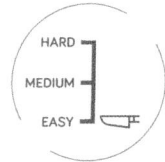  

Preparing the Vegetables

- 2 Large potatoes - Cyprus, King Edward or Maris Piper. Peel, rinse and cut into 4
- 1kg Combination of mixed fresh vegetables of your choice. Choose from courgettes, aubergines, carrots, closed cup mushrooms, cauliflower florets, peppers, cherry tomatoes, and red or white onions
- 160ml light olive oil
- 2-3 Large garlic cloves. Peel and slice
- 2-3 Sprigs fresh rosemary or 3 Tbsp dried oregano
- 1 Bay leaf
- Salt and freshly ground pepper
- 100ml Hot water

Cooking Method

1. Preheat fan oven to 280 -290 degrees C
2. Rinse and dry all vegetables of your choice accordingly. Aubergines, carrots, and onions need to be peeled. Trim and discard top and bottom stalks respectively. Discard the pith of peppers. If using tomatoes, add to the pan in the final 15 minutes of cooking time
3. Chop all the vegetables into large chunks of a similar size and place in a large mixing bowl
4. Add the potatoes and all the remaining ingredients, except the hot water to the bowl and mix with clean hands to evenly coat all the ingredients
5. Add them to a roasting tray or ovenproof dish
6. Pour the hot water into the mixing bowl and give it a swirl and then pour the contents into the roasting tray
7. Add a little more seasoning at this point if you feel you need to. Then roast until all the vegetables have shrivelled up and become very soft and are beginning to take on colour. If they brown before they are soft cover with foil and continue to roast

Serve with your favourite dip, warmed pitta breads and crumbled feta.

> **Top Tip.**
> The more the merrier! At least 3 colours and types of vegetables along with the potatoes for a great looking as well as tasting dish.

Μελιτζάνες
Στο
Φούρνο

Baked Aubergines with Garlic

Μελιτζάνες Στο Φούρνο

Aubergines are a firm favourite in my household. They have improved by far from the bitter, tough skinned varieties of old, which required salting to release their astringent juices. The speed and the simplicity of this dish adds to its appeal. I often add courgettes and peeled potatoes to make this stretch into a one-pot meal. Don't skimp on the garlic, as partnered with the sweet, fleshy aubergines, they truly complement each other well.

   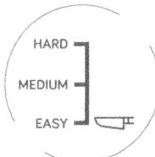  

Preparing the Aubergines

- 2 Large aubergines. Peel and cut in half lengthwise
- 1 Onion. Peel and finely chop
- 2 Large garlic cloves. Peel, cut into slices
- 4 Tbsp. light olive oil
- 200g Tin chopped tomatoes
- 1 Tsp dried oregano or dried mint
- ½ Tsp ground cinnamon
- Salt and freshly ground pepper to taste
- 200ml Water

Cooking Method

1. Preheat fan oven to 180 degrees C
2. Add the oil to a hot saucepan, stir in the onions, sauté for 2-3 minutes to soften, add the dried herbs and ground cinnamon, then stir in the chopped tomatoes
3. Lay the aubergines side by side in an ovenproof dish, pierce each one 4- 5 times, and insert a slice of garlic into each hole
4. Add the salt and pepper to the onions, pour this mixture over the aubergines., add the water to the pan to deglaze, and pour that into the ovenproof dish
5. Cover dish with foil and place in the oven until the aubergines are soft and yielding

Serve with tahini dip or grated cheese, Bulgur Wheat Pilaf, and bread of your choice.

Footnote.
Use aubergines as soon as they are peeled as they quickly discolour.

Φριτάτα

Greek Garden Frittata

Φρίτατα

Many Cypriot households would prepare this dish, in some form or other, after a long day. The variables would be determined more or less by the ingredients they have to hand or those they would purchase from the vans of the street vendors. The vendors, along with their recent harvests, would inch along the village streets full of that morning's yield using a megaphone announcing their produce for sale. It is a great dish to make when you have little or no time to prepare a meal and very few ingredients. Teach your children to make this and they will never go hungry.

   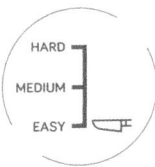  

Preparing the Frittata

- 1 Large potato. Peel, rinse, cut into 4 lengthwise, then slice crosswise as thinly as possible
- 2 Tomatoes. Rinse and discard core. Chop into dice
- 1 Small onion. Peel and finely chop. Alternatively, use 2 spring onions, trim stalks, rinse, pat dry and finely slice
- 1 Cupful of rinsed and dried spinach (optional)
- 4-6 Large eggs. Beaten and season eggs with salt and pepper.
- 4- 5 Tbsp light olive oil
- 1 Tsp dried oregano or marjoram, thyme, basil or dill (smell the herb and choose the one you are drawn to)
- 80g Greek feta cheese or vegan alternative, crumbled (optional)
- 2 Large cups of any combination of the following :
- 1 Small courgette. Discard stalk and trim the end. Slice lengthwise and cut into thin half moons
- ½ Red pepper. Discard pith and seeds and dice
- Closed cup mushrooms. Rinse, dry, trim stalks, and cut in quarters
- Asparagus. Gently bend the end of the asparagus to break off the tough end. Rinse and cut into 3-4 pieces.

Cooking Method

1. Preheat oven (if you would like to finish dish in the oven). Add oil to a large dry hot frying pan on a medium to high heat

2. Stir in the onions and sauté for 1-2 minutes. Turn down heat to medium, add potatoes, and cook for 3-4 minutes until they begin to colour on both sides and soften

3. Stir in the courgettes and sauté for 3-4 minutes or until they are golden brown on both sides

4. Stir in the chopped tomatoes. Cook until soft and then add the remaining vegetables (spinach last) and continue to cook until they are as soft as you like them

5. Stir in the dried herbs and add salt and pepper to taste. Add a drop more oil if the pan is dry

6. Pour in the seasoned beaten eggs and stir with a spatula to mix evenly in and around the vegetables. Essentially, you are scrambling them. When the eggs are nearly cooked to your liking, turn off heat and allow eggs to finish cooking in the residual heat of the pan. Add the crumbled feta and serve

7. Or, if you prefer your dish to look like an omelette, pour the beaten eggs in at step 6 and allow them to set a little around the edges of the pan. Then add the crumbled feta, using a spatula. Gently push the cooked portion towards the centre, tilting and rotating pan to let the runny eggs flow into the spaces. Finish in the oven for 3-5 minutes or until the eggs are set, but not hard.

Serve with black olives and crusty bread or toasted & buttered bread.

> **Top Tip.**
> Do not overcook eggs. They will continue to cook in the residual heat of the pan.

Σπανακόπιτα

Scrumptious Spanakopita Or Spinach pie

Σπανακόπιτα

The 'Spanakopita' is probably one of the single most well-known dishes from the Greek islands. If you have not tried it, you must. This tasty pie encapsulates those memories of sunnier climes in the layers of flaky filo pastry, spinach, and feta cheese. Over the years, I have tried out many recipes (I know, poor me!) and this is one of the simplest and tastiest versions. So, give it a try, as it so versatile and goes well with almost everything. It can also be a quick meal served with a dressed tomato salad.

  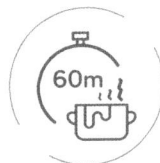 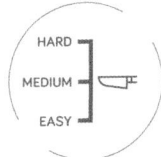  

Preparing the Spanakopita

Spinach Filling

- 260-300g Fresh spinach, washed, drained, wilted, and cooled
- 30g Flat leaf parsley. Rinse, drain and finely chop

and

- 100 grams Spring onions. Discard outer leaves and most of the green stalks, wash and finely chop

or

- 1 Large onion. Peeled and finely chop

and

- 2 garlic cloves. Peeled and minced
- 2 Tbsp light olive oil or butter
- 4 Eggs, beaten
- 285g Greek feta cheese
- 60g Grated aged halloumi
- 2 Tsp dried dill or 10g chopped fresh dill
- 1/2 Tsp ground cinnamon
- 1/2 Tsp dried mint
- 1/2 Tsp freshly grated nutmeg
- Zest of 1 lemon, unwaxed (rinse before you grate)
- Salt and freshly ground pepper to taste

- To wilt spinach, simply place warm spinach in a warm pan on a low heat. Stir and push down with a spatula

For the Filo Pastry Crust

- 270g (12-14 sheets) Ready-made chilled filo pastry. (Frozen will do; defrost thoroughly before you start the dish)
- 1 Cup light olive oil. You can use melted butter or a neutral cooking oil

You will need an ovenproof dish 9" X 13" (give or take) an inch either side.

Cooking Method

Filling

1. Squeeze out all the moisture from your cooled wilted spinach using clean hands or a clean tea towel
2. Sauté the onion/spring onions, garlic, cinnamon/nutmeg and pinch of salt and pepper in the light olive oil/butter on a low heat for 2-3 minutes. Take care not to colour the onions
3. Transfer the onion to a bowl to cool for a few minutes
4. Roughly chop the spinach and add it the bowl of cooked onion. Mix it in well. Add the dill, grated lemon zest, and the grated halloumi. Mix well to evenly distribute the ingredients
5. Crumble in the feta cheese and stir through
6. If all the ingredients in the bowl are cool, stir in the beaten eggs

Assembly of dish

Retain the filo pastry in its packaging until ready to use, then remove and cover with a damp towel as it dries out very quickly

1. Grease your dish with oil or butter
2. Using 5 sheets of filo pastry, line the base of the dish and brush each sheet with with oil/margarine as you go along
3. Gently spread 1/3 of the spinach filling over the filo pastry taking care to cover the base and flatten the filling. Cover with one sheet of filo (do not brush with oil). Repeat this step twice more until you have used all the spinach
4. Take the remaining filo pastry, one sheet at a time, brush each with oil and continue to layer on top of the filling. Repeat until you have used all the pastry
5. Tuck in or roll together any filo that is overhanging, brush with more oil, and sprinkle a few drops of water on to the surface of the spanakopita
6. Using a sharp knife, cut triangle, diamond, or square shapes into the top layers of filo taking care not to cut through to the filling

7. Bake in oven for 45 minutes at 180 degrees C, then turn down to low and cook for a further 15 minutes, or until the 'spanakopita' is crisp and golden brown all over. Remove from the oven and allow to cool for a few minutes before using your previous lines as a guide to cut all the way through. Eat hot or at room temperature. Chill any leftovers

Vegan Spanokopita Recipe

Follow the vegetarian recipe but swap the cheeses in the spinach filling with a vegan alternative. Omit the eggs and use olive oil instead of butter.

Leftovers are great in lunchboxes.

Top Tip.
Practise in advance the shape you like on a piece of paper, before you score your spanakopita.

Footnote.
You can make individual spanakopites using the same recipe and procedure simply take a couple of sheets of filo at a time, fill them and shape them like samosas or any shape and size you like.

Κρέπες με Σπανάκι

Special Spinach Pancakes

Κρέπες με Σπανάκι

We Cypriots have a recipe for pancakes called 'Kattimerka'. These, unlike traditional pancakes, are made with a dough, which takes a great deal longer to prepare and to cook. We have, therefore, naturally taken to making a traditional pancake batter, as it is far simpler and quicker to make. Nevertheless, the filling for these pancakes is authentically Greek and simply delicious. Our equivalent to pancake day is called 'Clean Monday', which heralds the beginning of lent and of forty days of fasting. We have annual family beach celebrations and a pescatarian banquet on this day. I am confident that, once you try this recipe, you will not wait for Pancake Day to come round to make these savoury-filled pancakes, as they are a great tasting brunch or quick supper dish.

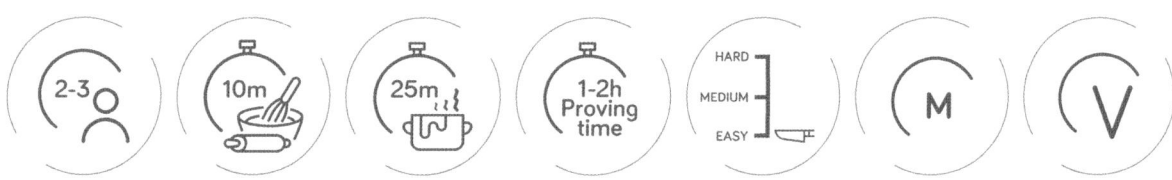

Preparing the Pancakes

Vegetarian

Pancake Batter 4-6 Pancakes

- 340ml Cold milk
- 4 Eggs, beaten
- 170g Plain flour
- Pinch of salt
- Oil, butter or margarine for frying

Filling

- 150g Spinach. Rince and dry
- 3 Tbsp Greek yoghurt
- 2 Eggs, room temperature
- 6 Tbsp grated halloumi (or parmesan)
- ½ Tsp ground mint
- Salt and freshly ground pepper to taste
- ½ Tsp ground cinnamon (optional)

Cooking Method

1. Preheat fan oven to a medium heat - 190-210 degrees C
2. Put all the ingredients for the pancake batter in a bowl and mix until you have a smooth batter. Place in fridge for 1-2 hrs
3. Wilt the spinach in a pan with a drop of oil or butter, take off the heat, and pour into a sieve to drain and cool a little
4. Preheat a frying pan on a medium/high heat. Add a drop of oil or a knob of butter and swirl to cover the base of the pan. Add a small ladle full of batter at a time and let the batter coat the base of the pan. Fry for 2-3 minutes on each side. Repeat until all the batter has been used. Put pancakes to one side
5. Add the spinach to a mixing bowl, add ¾ of the grated halloumi, ¾ of the yogurt, ground cinnamon, salt and pepper and mix well
6. Stir in the eggs and mix well. The spinach should be cool/warm but not hot. If the mixture is not slightly fluid, stir in the remaining yoghurt
7. Divide the filling equally between all the pancakes and roll them into a cigar shape and place side by side, tucking the ends under, and place in oven proof dish. Add a dot of butter to each pancake and the remaining grated cheese, and oven bake until heated through and beginning to colour

Footnote.
If your filling is very fluid, simply spread all over each pancake before rolling. It firms up in the oven.

> **Top Tip.**
> Make pancake batter in advance and place in a jug covered with cling film. It can keep for up to 24 hours in the fridge. Stir before using.

Πατάτες
Γιαχνί

Yummy Potatoes Yiachni

Πατάτες Γιαχνί

'Yiachni' means to stew in tomato, onion, and olive oil. Do not be fooled by the simple ingredients in this dish. It is a traditional and age-old method of cooking vegetables, which transforms the most simple dishes from the everyday mundane to something really quite special. Carried out in a thoroughly Greek manner, this is low effort, maximum flavour. Cypriot potatoes are grown on family farms. The skin is slightly red, and, as the soil they are grown in is so high in minerals, they are superior in both taste and nutrients. I spent many a summer picking potatoes by hand - back-breaking work that I do not care to repeat. Use a Cypriot potato variety if you can, as they are the main ingredient in this one-pot versatile dish, which is easy and delicious, Cypriots cook their vegetables until they are soft which also allows them to take on the flavourings they are cooked with.

   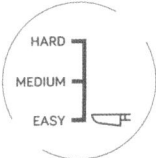  

Preparing the Yiachni

- 1 kg Potatoes. Use a variety such as Cyprus, Maris Piper, King Edward or Red Rooster. Peel, rinse and cut each into 4 pieces
- 2 Onions. Peeled and roughly chopped
- 300g Tomato pasatta or chopped tinned tomatoes
- 1 Tsp tomato purée
- 1 Tsp ground cinnamon
- 1 Vegetable/vegan stock cube. Dissolved
- Salt and freshly ground pepper
- 1 ½ Pints of hot water (rough guide)

Cooking Method

1. Heat a large pan on a medium heat add the oil. Heat, add the onions, and sauté for 2-3 minutes or until they take on a little colour and are soft. Stir frequently
2. Stir in the tomatoes, tomato purée, and ground cinnamon. Add the potatoes to the pan and stir well, so as to coat them in the oil and tomatoes
3. Dissolve the stock in the hot water and pour into the pan. The water should just cover the potatoes. Adjust the amount of water if necessary
4. Season and turn down to a medium heat and cook with a lid until the potatoes are completely soft
5. Throughout the cooking time, gently shake the pan from side to side to prevent potatoes from sticking to pan. This also helps to mix the flavours

Serve with crusty bread.

Footnote.
You can use this recipe to make any combination of 'Yiachni' dishes. Frozen peas, green beans, chunks of peeled carrot, or a combination of all of these can be added on top of the potatoes. You can also cook the vegetables in this way without the potatoes. Greeks commonly cook artichokes this way too. The recipe is as follows on the next page.

Αγκινάρες
Γιαχνί

Artichokes Yiachni

Αγκινάρες Γιαχνί

Artichokes are indigenous to Cyprus and surrounding Mediterranean countries. This recipe is yet another prime example of how Cypriots can transform a recipe using an ingredient as humble as a thistle into a succulent-tasting and satin-smooth dish. Daunting as the prospect of preparing artichokes may be, it is an easy recipe with just 4 ingredients. Artichokes are culinarily twin of iron supplements. Our elders always advised us to replace prescriptions for iron with the consumption of artichokes for those who are anaemic. I echo this to my children to this day.

  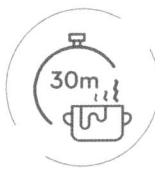 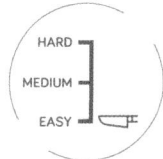  

Preparing the Yiachni

- 3-4 Fresh whole artichokes
- 400g Chopped tinned tomatoes
- 1 Large onion. Peel and finely chop
- 3 Tbsp light olive oil
- ½ Tsp ground cinammon
- Salt and freshly ground pepper to taste

Top Tip.
You can eat artichoke raw. Prepare as above and shower with lemon juice, or nibble on the leaves at the base, breaking off one at a time, just as Greeks do.

Cooking Method

How to prepare an artichoke

Trim end of stem and discard. Cut off the remaining stem close to the base of the artichoke, cut in half, and peel the fibrous outer part of the stalk to reveal the cylindrical tender core. Immerse them in cold water, with a drop of lemon juice to prevent discolouring.

Place the artichoke head on its side on a chopping board, cut off the tops of the leaves, roughly 1/3 above the thick base and discard the leaves

Discard all outer leaves by pulling them off one at a time until you get to the pale mint-green tender centre leaves. Grab hold of these and pull them to remove in one go. These are great to nibble on or discard

Take a teaspoon and scrape out the furry centre, retaining as much of the remaining artichoke heart as possible

Rinse the artichoke

Sparingly, trim off any remaining fibrous dark green pieces on the underside of the artichoke heart

Cut the heart in ½ or ¼ and add them to the water along with the stems

Repeat until all the artichokes are prepared.

1. Heat a saucepan on a medium heat, add the oil, heat, and stir in the onions, sauté until they are soft and translucent
2. Stir in the cinnamon, follow quickly with the tomatoes and cook for 1-2 minutes
3. Stir in the artichokes and coat with tomatoes. Season to taste
4. Add cold water to just cover the artichokes
5. Cook on a medium heat until tender, but holding their shape

Κυρία
Πιάτα

Mains

Ντολμάδες

Delectable Dolmades

Ντολμάδες

'Dolmades' or stuffed vine leaves, as they are commonly known, are named 'Koubebia' by Cypriots. They normally contain mince, although this fasting version of the recipe is equally as good. A long list of countries from the Balkans, Turkic and Middle East through to Central Asia all have variations of these vine leaf-wrapped savoury parcels of fragrant rice. Loved by all, we home cooks each have our own coveted ratio of ingredients which we use at some time or other. We prepare these and serve boastfully. I recount this recipe somewhat nostalgically, as they where my dearly-departed father's favourite. He was very particular about his recipe and liked it faintly tinted with tomato, glowing with lemon juice, and healthily radiant with parsley. If ever there was an original plant-based dish, then this would be it.

Cooking Method

1. Blanche the vine leaves in hot water for 4-5 minutes. This will remove the brine and soften the leaves.
   Remove from hot water, and immerse in cold water to stop cooking, and also enable you to handle them
2. Heat the light olive oil on a medium heat, add the onions and sauté for 3-4 minutes or until they soften and begin to colour. Stir often so they cook evenly
3. Stir in the dry herbs, spices, and tomato purée
4. Stir in the chopped fresh tomatoes and cook for 2-3 minutes
5. Turn off the heat and add all the chopped fresh herbs. Stir until they wilt
6. Add the rice and ¾ of the lemon juice, extra virgin olive oil, and salt and pepper to taste. Stir until all the ingredients are evenly incorporated. Leave to one side
7. Drain the vine leaves. Take one leaf at a time, lay it flat on a large plate with the shiny side facing down, snip off the stalk with scissors, and discard
8. Place one tbsp of the filling at the wider part of the vine leaf near the stalk. Fold over from the top onto the vine leaf and then fold in either side onto vine leaf, tucking the filling into the leaf as you roll the vine on to itself to form a tightly packed cylinder. Place one layer of ripped or small vine leaves on the base of the pan before adding the rolled dolmades. Place the dolmades in the saucepan as you go along
9. Place in a saucepan. Start at the outer edge and lie them lengthwise side by side, following the outer edge of the pan and working inwards to the centre. Layer on top of each other, Repeat until all the dolmades are finished. Place a tight fitting plate or saucer right way down on top of the dolmades. Weigh it down by sitting a large mug filled with water on to it
10. Add the water and lemon juice to the pan, in which you made the filling. Stir it to deglaze. Do not heat and pour the stock in to the pan of dolmades
11. Put the dolmades on to boil on a medium heat for 12-15 minutes or until it is gently bubbling. Put the weight/mug to one side whilst you gently tilt the pan from side to side. Place weight back on top and continue to cook on a very low heat for 40 minutes. Tilt the pan side to side frequently during cooking
12. Remove weight, tilt the pan and check the liquid, lift the plate with a fork. If the liquid has been absorbed, add 50ml more and put back on a very low heat for 10 minutes more. Do not let the dolmades boil dry. Do not put the weight back on the dolmades
13. Turn off heat, put a lid on the pan, and allow the dolmades to rest for 15 minutes, so as to absorb any residual liquid before you serve

Preparing the Dolmades

- 300g Vine leaves in brine (drained weight)
- 150g Long grain rice. Rinsed, drained in a sieve, and leave to one side
- 2 Large onions. Peel and finely chop
- 30g Flat leaf parsley. Rinse and pat dry
- 2 Large ripe tomatoes. Decore and remove skin
- 15g Fresh mint. Rinsed, pat dry. Finely sliced
- 15g Fresh dill. Rinse, pat dry and finely chop. Alternatively, 1 Tsp dried dill
- 1 Tbsp tomato purée
- 2 Large lemons, juiced with no pips
- 1 Tsp ground cinnamon
- 1 Tsp dry mint
- 1 Tsp dry oregano
- 40ml Light olive oil
- 40ml Extra virgin olive oil
- Salt and freshly ground pepper to taste
- 450ml Water

> **Top Tip.**
> If you find cooking the dolmades on the stove top daunting, follow the same recipe, but pack them into an oven proof dish and bake in a preheated medium oven covered in foil, shiny side down, for 55-60 minutes. Ensure they do not cook dry. Allow them to rest for 15 minutes or so before serving.

Footnote.
If you find the raw mix is too fluid to roll, place a sieve over the pan of rolled koubebia, and pour the mix in to the sieve, allowing most of the liquid to drain into the koubebia. Then continue to roll the vine leaves and add them to the pan. In either case, you need to pour back all the liquid to the pan of rolled koubebia, as this is where the flavour is.

Μπριάμ
Στο
Φούρνο

Baked Briam Vegetables

Μπριάμ Στο Φούρνο

It is thought that the word 'briam' is derived from the Turkish word 'biryam', which means roasted vegetables. Persia has a similar dish called 'biryan', which is roasted food with rice. India also has 'biryani', which again is a slow-cooked rice dish, Cyprus has a version of a slow-baked vegetable dish, which we serve with rice, and call 'briam'. It is an upmarket vegetable dish that is presented beautifully and is great for when appearances count. Use your best oven-to-table dish for this, if you would like to present this dish straight from the oven.

  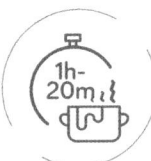 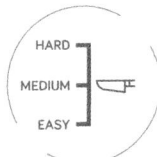  

Preparing the Vegetables

- 3 Medium sized potatoes. Use Cyprus, King Edward, Red Rooster. Peeled and placed in a bowl of cold water
- 3 Large courgettes. Rinse, trim top and bottom stalks, and leave to one side
- 2 Large aubergines. Peel and leave to one side
- 3 Large ripe tomatoes. Rinse and discard core
- 400g Tinned chopped tomatoes
- 2 Large red or white onions. Peel and slice into rounds
- 30g Flat leaf parsley. Rinsed, dry and finely chop
- 160g Light olive oil
- 50ml Hot water
- 4 Garlic cloves. Peel and mince
- 2 Tsp dried oregano
- Salt and freshly ground pepper

Cooking Method

You will need a deep 10" circular oven-to-table dish

1. Preheat fan oven to 190-210 degrees C
2. Slice aubergines crosswise into 2-3 cm thick rounds. Place in a large mixing bowl
3. Slice the courgettes crosswise into 1-2 cm thick rounds Add to the bowl
4. Slice the tomatoes into 2-3 cm thick rounds. Leave to one side
5. Slice the onions crosswise into 1 cm thick rounds. Leave to one side
6. Slice the potatoes crosswise into 1-2 cm thick rounds. Add to the bowl
7. Add the oil, minced garlic, parsley, salt, pepper, and oregano to the bowl and mix all the vegetables with clean hands. Evenly coat all the vegetables in the oil and seasonings
8. Take a large shallow oven-to-table (preferably a round one) and spread ½ of the chopped tinned tomatoes into the base. Season very lightly
9. Begin placing all the vegetables into the dish, starting with the potatoes, and then alternate all the vegetables in order to include the onion rounds and tomatoes from the outside edge of the dish, rotating and overlapping onto the other like a snails shell. Repeat until all the vegetables have been used. You are looking for vegetables to be tightly packed. You can do this in two layers if you have vegetables left over or only have a small ovenproof dish
10. Pour the hot water into the bowl. Shake gently to mix all the remaining oil and seasonings before pouring evenly into the dish
11. Evenly spread the remaining tinned tomatoes and juices over the vegetables and cover with foil, shiny side down.
12. Remove the foil for the last 20-25 minutes turning oven down to medium. Remove from oven when the vegetables have wilted, softened, absorbed all the liquid, and have taken on a little colour

Serve with rice, crusty bread, and olives and/or crumbled feta.

> **Top Tip.**
> You can prepare this in advance, complete the dish up to step 12 and then bake when required.

Ντοματοκεφτέδες

No Meat Tomato Balls

Ντοματοκεφτέδες

Fried patties are a very retro recipe that went to the back of the cupboard and was forgotten about. It is high time that this underrated dish was rediscovered. 'Keftedes' simply means balls/patties, the preceding word references the primary ingredient, which, in this case is tomatoes- 'ντομάτες'. However, the recipe for meatballs, which incorporates meat are known as 'Keftedes'. This recipe mixes up meal times the Cypriot way, and produces a healthy, savoury, and satisfying patty, full of hidden goodness. These are shallow fried and make a really delicious vegan meal. I can assure you they will be snapped up by all. My tip is to make more than you need.

   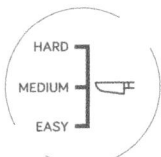  

Preparing the Tomato Balls

- 500g Large ripe, firm tomatoes. Discard core and chop into small dice
- 1 Large courgette. Rinse and discard top and bottom stalks. Place a box grater on a plate, grate courgette using the small side of box grater, and leave to one side
- 1 Medium sized potato. Peel, rinse, grate using the small side of the box grater, and put in a sieve to drain
- 1 Large red onion. Peel and finely chop
- 30g Flat leaf parsley Rinse, dry, finely chop stalks and all the leaves
- 1 Tsp dried mint
- 1 Tsp ground cumin
- 1 Tsp dried oregano
- 4-6 Tbsp breadcrumbs
- 1 Large egg, beaten (optional)
- 2 Tbsp self-raising flour
- Salt and freshly ground pepper to taste
- ¾ Cup light olive oil. For frying
- ¼ Cup vegetable oil. For frying

Top Tip.
Add a little more breadcrumbs at step 5, after you have chilled the mixture, if it is still too fluid.

Additional Tip.
You can make up the amount of vegetables required with any that you have to hand.

Footnote.
To check if your oil is hot enough to fry simply take a tiny pinch of the mixture and drop it into the oil, if it rises quickly to the top the oil is hot enough.

Cooking Method

1. Have a large mixing bowl to hand. Squeeze out all the moisture from the potato and the courgette with clean hands over the sink. Then put in a mixing bowl or wring out the moisture using a clean tea towel
2. Follow on into the bowl with all the remaining ingredients, except the egg and flour. Mix all the ingredients until really well combined
3. Stir in all the egg and breadcrumbs, and then the flour - 1 tbsp at a time, and mix well
4. Have a large plate to hand
5. Preheat a saucepan or deep frying pan on a very low heat. Do not add the frying oil. Whilst pan is heating, roll out your 'no meat' balls
6. Measure a tablespoonful of the mixture into your hand and use the palm of your hands to roll into balls or patties. If the mixture does not combine, chill for ½ an hour, then start again, placing balls on the plate. Repeat until the mixture is done
7. Add the oil to the pan and turn up heat to high. When hot, add the tomato balls one at a time, starting from the outer edge of the pan and going in a circular pattern until you get to the middle. Leave a little room between each so that they do not stick together. You may have to fry in batches. Ensure oil is halfway up the balls and hot so they do not break
8. Turn down heat to medium/high. After 5-6 minutes, check the first tomato ball. If it is nicely golden brown and holding its shape, turn over with a spoon, and repeat until you have fried them evenly on both sides. Do not undercook, as these taste much better when vegetables are cooked through. Turn down heat a little more if they are browning too much, before they are completely cooked through
9. Put them in a lined serving bowl with paper kitchen towel to absorb the excess oil. Discard it when you have finished cooking the tomato balls
10. Repeat step 7 until you have used all the mixture

Have your 'serve with' ready, as hands will help themselves to these just as soon as you have finished frying. Salad, dips, potato or sweet potato fries are all good accompaniments, and do not forget a fresh lemon wedge to squeeze over before eating.

Μπάμιες
γιαχνί

Beautiful Okra Ladies Fingers

Μπάμιες Γιαχνί

Okra, also known as 'ladies fingers' are a green vegetable that taste delicate sweet, and have a silky, creamy texture. The finished dish, however, can vary in taste depending on how the okra are cooked as they are so mild in flavour. I stew the okra in a tomato, onion, and olive oil sauce - known as 'yiachni', until the flavours merge and the okra melt in the mouth. It is believed that the Egyptians first cultivated okra in the 12th century, before introducing it to the Greeks, who deem it to be a supreme vegetable. Ethiopians roast the seeds of the okra and use them to brew coffee. Not many European countries are familiar with okra, probably as people are unsure how it should be prepared. Okra have an undeserved reputation for being 'slimy'. I beg to differ; they do require a level of skill and attention to prepare, but I highly recommend that you have a go. This recipe, the correct preparation, and a really tasty recipe, make the okra dish really very special.

   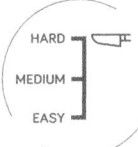 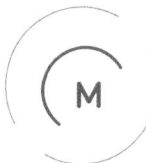 

Preparing the Okra

Pour the whole okra into a large bowl of cold water. Wash them and discard any that feel very fibrous. Pour them in a colander to drain. Then, place them in a large tray lined with a thick absorbent clean tea towel. Leave them to dry or 'marani' - 'Μαράνη' as we say, for 4-6 hrs. It is best to do this the night before you require them. Discard the stalks following the conical shape of the okra, by rotating a sharp knife with one hand, whilst holding the okra in the other hand. Do this is in order not to cut into the okra and expose the seeds. Repeat until all okra are done. Discard any okra that are hard or brittle. Do not rinse the okra after you have discarded the stalks. Do not discard any okra that you have cut into. Waste is unnecessary and it will not detract from the taste of the dish.

- 500g Fresh okra (prepared as above)

- 3-4 Large floury potatoes: such as Spunta, King Edward or Maris Piper. Peel, rinse, drain, and cut each into 3 pieces

- 300g Tomato passata or 400g chopped tinned tomatoes

- 1 Tsp tomato purée

- 2 Onions. Peel and roughly chop

- 4 Tbsp light olive oil

- ½ Tsp ground cinnamon

- Salt and Freshly ground pepper to taste

- 400ml Cold water or enough to just cover vegetables

Cooking Method

1. Add the oil to a preheated saucepan on a medium heat and stir in the onions. Add salt to taste at this stage to draw out the moisture of the onions so that they will take longer to brown and soften. This will enhance the flavour of the finished dish. Cook until the onions are really soft and beginning to brown

2. Stir in the cinnamon and follow with the tomato purée and pasatta

3. Add the potatoes to the base of the pan and then stir gently to coat with the onions

4. Pour in the okra. Do not stir.

5. Pour in the water. Season with salt and pepper to taste

6. Bring to the boil. Then gently tilt the pan from side to side to mix everything and to prevent ingredients from catching. Be careful to do this without breaking the delicate okra. Turn down heat to low. This is a stew-like dish and so should not boil dry. Add a little more water if necessary

7. Simmer gently until the okra are pliable, dark green in colour, and some start to reveal their seeds. Pierce a potato with a fork it to ensure the entire dish is properly cooked

8. Check the seasoning and adjust accordingly

Serve with crusty bread to mop up all the juices.

Top Tip.
Soft, soft, soft. Cook okra until they just begin to lose their shape. They will taste better for it.

Footnote.
If you cannot find fresh okra, use frozen Greek okra or the Asian varieties are just as good. Add still frozen to the pan at step 3.

Crispy Tempura Okra

Τραγανές Μπάμιες

Fried okra is another method of cooking okra, which is similar to tempura vegetables. I use corn meal, also known as corn maize, and then coat in semolina, which gives the okra a crisper bite.

Cooking Method

Prepare the Crispy Tempura Okra the same way as the Beautiful Okra Ladies Fingers. Directions above on page 60.

1. Make a thin batter using cornflour maize or plain flour mixed with water, until you have the consistency you like. Add salt and pepper to batter

or

2. Dip okra into an emollient, such as aquafaba (drained juice from tinned chickpeas), beaten egg, milk, plain yoghurt or buttermilk

3. Heat some neutral oil in a frying pan on a medium high heat

4. Dip the okra into the batter or emollient and then add some salt and pepper to a bowl of semolina, and coat each okra well

5. Shallow fry the okra for 4-6 minutes or until they are soft in the centre and crisp on the outside, turning halfway through the cooking time. Repeat until all the okra are cooked

Serve with rice, bulgur wheat pilaf, or orzo pasta, and a Greek salad, with warmed pita breads and skordalia dip.

Top Tip.
If using frozen okra ensure they are thoroughly defrosted & drained before using in this recipe.

Footnote.
You can also coat Greek feta cheese or vegan feta, and most vegetables, and cook in the same way. You may also replace the corn flour with fine semolina, plain flour or rice flour.

Μουσακάς

Moreish Meatless Moussaka

Μουσακάς

Moussaka - no Greek cook book would not be complete without a version of this beloved dish. I have adapted this classic and made it suitable for vegans, although I have not gone down the route of using a meat substitute, as I feel it would be a step too far away from the integrity of the original dish. Instead, I have replaced the traditional mince layer with mushrooms. Additionally I have remained closer still to the essence of the dish with my choice of herbs, spices, and the triple layer of vegetables - all topped off with a non-dairy, yet delightfully creamy, bechamel sauce. This is a splendid get-together dinner recipe with a touch of luxury, which will have everyone eagerly waiting for you to dish up.

  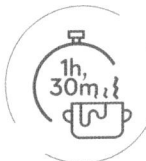 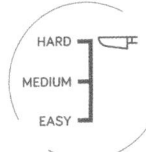 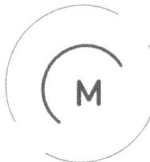 

Preparing the Moussaka

You will need a deep ovenproof dish 13" x 10" x 3" deep

Base layer

- 3-4 Large potatoes. Peel and sliced lengthwise into scollops, roughly the thickness of your thumb, and then place in a bowl of cold water
- 3 Large aubergines. Discard stalks and peel. Slice lengthwise at a similar thickness to the scolloped potatoes
- 3 Large courgettes. Discard top and bottom stalks. Slice lengthwise of a similar thickness to the potatoes
- ½ Cup of light olive oil for frying

Meatless Mince Layer

- 2 Large onions. Peel and roughly chop
- 500g Closed cup white or chestnut mushrooms Quickly toss in a bowl of cold water to dislodge any soil and put in a colander to drain. Trim stalks, cut in half, and then cut into thick slices. Put to one side
- 400g Tinned chopped tomatoes
- 2 Large cloves of garlic. Peel and mince
- 30g Light olive oil or a neutral cooking oil
- ½ Tbsp ground cinnamon
- 1 Tbsp dried mint
- 1 Tbsp tomato purée

- 50ml Red wine suitable for vegans, or water
- 1 Vegetable stock cube suitable for vegans (dissolve in the wine)
- Salt and freshly ground pepper to taste

Béchamel layer

- 1½ Litres fresh milk or oat or almond milk
- 150g Plain flour
- 150g Light olive oil
- 1 Egg, beaten. Omit for vegan recipe
- 1 Heaped tsp English mustard
- Salt to taste and a pinch of ground white pepper
- 100g Extra mature cheddar cheese, grated. Alternatively, use vegan alternative
- 100g Red Leicester, grated. Alternatively, use vegan alternative

Cooking Method

Preparing the base layer

1. Drain the scolloped potatoes
2. Line 2-3 Large baking trays with foil, shiny side up, and grease the foil. Lay all the aubergines and courgette onto the trays and season very lightly with salt and pepper. Roast in oven for about 12-15 minutes or until the vegetables are soft and cooked. They do not need to colour
3. Preheat a frying pan. Add the oil on a medium-high heat, pat dry the scolloped potatoes, and fry on each side for 3-4 minutes or until golden brown, but still firm in centre. Repeat until you have fried all the potatoes. Then place them on a plate lined with a kitchen towel to drain excess oil. Turn off heat
4. Check vegetables, remove from oven, and leave to one side. Turn off oven

Meatless Mince Layer

1. Heat a saucepan. Add the oil allocated to the meatless mince layer plus the oil from the pan you fried the potatoes in, on a medium-high heat. Add the onions and cook until they are soft for 2-3 minutes, turn up heat, and stir in the mushrooms. Cook for 2 minutes
2. Turn down heat to medium and stir in the wine/stock. Let the alcohol cook out for a minute or two
3. Stir in the minced garlic followed by the chopped tomatoes and the tomato purée
4. Add the chopped mushrooms
5. Then stir in the ground cinnamon, dried mint, oregano, salt and freshly-ground pepper to taste. Adjust seasoning accordingly. Allow to cook on a medium heat for 15 minutes then take off the heat

Assembling the dish

Preheat fan oven 180-190 degrees C

1. Cover the base of the ovenproof dish with the pre-cooked potato scollops, laying them side by side, and overlap where necessary, so that there are no gaps. Take the potatoes into the corners and up to the sides
2. Layer the aubergines side by side over the potatoes, overlapping them so that there are no gaps - up to the sides and corners of the dish

3. In the opposite direction to the aubergines, cover the aubergines with the courgettes, again side by side, overlapping them up to the sides and corners of the dish
4. Pour the meatless mince layer onto the vegetables. Use a spatula to spread over the vegetables as evenly as possible up to the corners and sides. Take care to cover them completely. Flatten and press down firmly with the spatula, so that you have an even surface
5. Take a knife and carefully pierce the vegetables in 5-6 different areas of the dish. This will allow the juices to seep through and give you a firmer base for the Béchamel Sauce and give the vegetables more flavour. Leave to one side whilst you make the sauce

Béchamel sauce

Have all the measured ingredients and the utensils to hand before you begin. You will need a medium saucepan, a hand balloon whisk, and a spatula.

1. Preheat fan oven to 190 degrees C
2. Add the flour to a saucepan. Put on a low to medium heat and whisk in the oil until it's a smooth paste. Let it cook out for one minute. Whisk
3. Whisk in half of the milk and continue to stir until the sauce thickens, turn down heat to low, then add the remaining milk and continue to stir until it begins to bubble
4. Stir in ¾ of the grated cheese and, when it is melted, turn off the heat. Stir in the mustard
5. Whisk in the beaten egg in very quickly. Whisk in a pinch of salt and a pinch of pepper. Taste and adjust seasoning if necessary
6. Pour the béchamel sauce over the top of the dish. Use the spatula to scrape the sides of the pan clean and to even out the sauce, covering the surface of the dish
7. Sprinkle the remaining grated cheese over the sauce
8. Let the dish stand for 15 minutes before you bake, so that it sets a little
9. Bake in oven until it is bubbling and evenly golden brown all over. Check after 40 minutes by piercing the centre with a sharp knife. There should be little resistance from the vegetables. If not, continue to bake
10. Remove dish from the oven and allow it cool for 60 minutes, so that it sets, to allow you to portion nicely

Serve with a Greek salad, pickles, and any olives you like.

Top Tip.
Make in individual dishes if you would like to serve straight from the oven.

Trouble shooting
Read through your ingredients of choice, such as the vegan cheese, and ensure they are suitable for use in cooking and can be grated.

Footnote.
Refrigerate, if making well in advance. Take out of the fridge 10-15 minutes before baking. Cover with foil whilst baking in the oven and remove foil for the final 15-20 minutes of cooking. This gives more time to brown the dish.

κουνουπίδι
κρασάτο

Celebrated Cauliflower & Red Wine Stew

Κουνουπίδι Κρασάτο

Cauliflower-'Κουνουπίδι' is a harvest which was originally indigenous to Cyprus. Krassato-'Κρασάτο' is to stew in wine. This is the recipe of all recipes and absolutely like no other stew you have ever tasted. This tastes aromatic, fruity, and full-bodied like the wine you marinade and cook it in. Cyprus is one of the oldest wine-making countries in the world and this dish echoes that skill. Perfected over centuries, and imitated by many dishes such as Coq au vin or Beef bourguignon, this is the Cypriot original. I am fiercely guarded about my vegan adaptation of this recipe and have not passed it on- even to my children. Until now, when thought it was high time to share it. Make this dish when you want to impress, spoil, or celebrate.

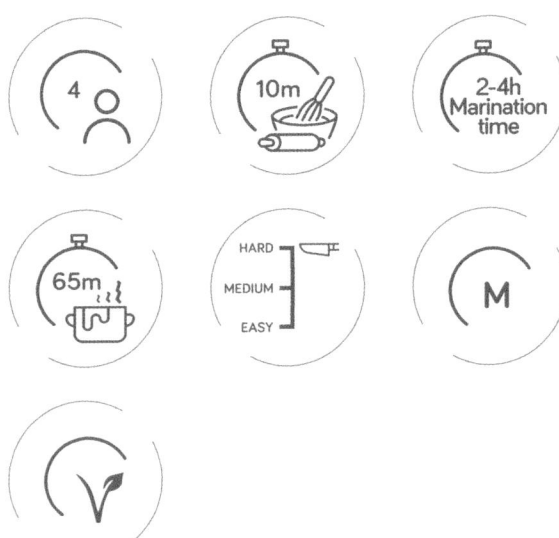

Preparing the Stew

- 2 Cauliflowers. Very large
- 4-6 Large potatoes, such as Spunta, Desiree, King Edward or Maris Piper
- 650ml Red dry fruity wine. 'Othello' or 'Keo' are authentic Greek wines
- 1 Large piece of cassia bark (not cinnamon stick)
- 200ml Vegetable oil or other neutral cooking oil
- 1 Vegetable stock cube suitable for vegans
- 500ml Cold water
- ½ Lemon, juiced
- Salt and freshly ground pepper to taste

Top Tip.
It is fine to mix 2-3 red wines for this dish if you have open bottles in the cupboard. You could even use some rosé. Do not use sparkling wines.

Cooking Method

1. Pour the wine into a large mixing bowl
2. Peel the potatoes. Rinse, cut each into 3 pieces, and place them in the bowl of wine
3. Discard the leaves of the cauliflower, rinse and cut each in half, place them on top of the potatoes in bowl of wine
4. Allow to marinade, turning the vegetables every 20-25 minutes so that they marinade as evenly as possible. If marinading for more than 2 hrs, place the bowl in the fridge
5. After marinading, place a large colander in another bowl and put all the vegetables through it to drain off the excess wine. Save the wine from both bowls
6. Heat the oil in a saucepan on a medium heat. When the oil is hot, sear the potatoes on all sides until golden brown but, not soft in the centre. The trick is not to crowd the pan or the oil temperature will drop. Repeat until all potatoes are done. Place them in a large saucepan as you go along
7. Sear the cauliflower on all sides until golden brown, but not soft. Repeat until all the cauliflower is done. Place on a plate lined with paper kitchen towel to absorb most of the excess oil. Drain off excess oil for 5 minutes before adding the cauliflower on top of the potatoes, stalk side down
8. Pour the oil from the saucepan into a pan to cool, so that you may discard it when it cools. Add the wine/marinade from both bowls into the pan and gently heat through on a low heat
9. Stir with a wooden spoon to deglaze the pan. When it starts to simmer, pour in the water
10. Place a sieve onto the vegetables and pour the wine through it into the pan of cauliflower. Juice the lemon into the pan over the sieve to catch any pips
11. Add the stock, cassia bark, lemon juice, salt and pepper to taste. The liquid level should come half way up to the cauliflower. If not, add a little more water
12. Bring the pan of vegetables to boil on a medium heat, then turn down to low, and continue to simmer until the vegetables are soft in the centre, but holding their shape. Gently shake the pan from side to side 3-4 times throughout the cooking time to prevent sticking. Do not let the dish cook dry. Add a little more water if necessary
13. Gently pierce a potato with a fork to see if the dish is ready. Taste a little of the liquid before serving and adjust seasoning accordingly. Let it stand with the lid on for 10 minutes before serving

Serve with a dressed salad and crusty bread.

Κολοκάσι
Γιάχνι

Taro and Tomato Yiachni

Κολοκασι Γιάχνι

'Taro' or 'Colocassi' - originally the Latin name, but still used in Cyprus today, is a root vegetable that has a starchy, nutty taste and a satisfyingly dense texture. Cypriot landowners utilise most of the cultivable land for farming and agricultural purposes. Taro has been a popular harvest both as a staple food ingredient and as a valued commodity to sell for years. It looks like a long potato, although the peel and texture of the flesh are more similar to a sweet potato. Taro is mostly used as an alternative to potato in meat dishes and can be prepared in many ways, I have included potato in this dish to bulk it out and to produce a more usual and palatable flavour for those who are not familiar with these new ingredients. You must peel taro, and it cannot be eaten raw. It is typically cooked along with celery, as the sweetness of the celery balances the nuttiness of the taro perfectly. This is another family favourite, which is popular with children. When I come across this, I prepare it with great enthusiasm, gently stewing it in tomato, olive oil, and onions. This method is known as 'Yiachni'.

   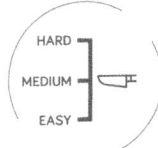  

Preparing the Yiachni

- 1 -1 ¼ Kg or 2-3 large taro. Taro will feel firm if they are fresh and will not have soft bits
- 2 Large potatoes. Peel, rinse, and cut each into 3 pieces
- 2 Large onions Peel and roughly chop
- 3 Celery stalks (with leaves if possible)
- 400g Chopped tinned tomatoes or 400g tomato pasatta
- 600ml Cold water
- 200ml Vegetable oil
- 4 Tbsp light olive oil
- 1 Tbsp tomato purée
- ½ Tsp ground cinnamon
- ½ Lemon, juiced
- Salt and lots of freshly ground pepper

Prepare the taro as follows:

Place a thick chopping board on a tea towel

Holding the taro firmly, put it on the chopping board, cut off white stalk, and discard

Stand the taro on flat cut end, and peel

Once peeled, rinse, and dry with a clean kitchen towel, as they become slippery when wet

Holding the taro with a tea towel, take a short, strong, knife, cut in, and crack/snap pieces off that are roughly the same size - a little larger than tea lights

Cooking Method

1. Heat both of the oils in the same saucepan on a medium to high heat
2. Sear the taro pieces on all sides until they soften and begin to colour. Do not crowd the pan, as the temperature of the oil will drop. Add the seared taro to another large saucepan as you go along. Repeat until all the taro is seared and colour the potatoes on all sides until golden brown but not soft in the centre. Then, add to the pan on top of the taro
3. Place ¾ of the hot oil into a small pan to cool and be discarded later. Add the onions to the remaining oil and sauté until evenly golden brown and soft
4. Stir the tomato purée into the onions, quickly followed by the chopped tomatoes, cinnamon, and a generous amount of freshly ground pepper. Cook for a 1-2 minutes
5. Pour the raw chopped celery into the pan of taro
6. Pour the sautéed onion/tomatoes on top of celery
7. Stir the vegetable stock into the pan in which you sautéed the onion/tomato, and stir with a wooden spoon to deglaze the pan. After 1-2 minutes, pour the stock into the pan of taro, add more water if the stock does not reach half way up to the potatoes
8. Add the lemon juice, salt, and a small sprinkling of pepper to taste
9. Bring to the boil, then turn down heat. Gently shake the pan from side to side 4-5 times during cooking time to prevent the contents from sticking, to mix the ingredients, and to check the fluidity of the stew
10. Simmer until the taro and the vegetables are extremely tender to bite, adjust seasoning if necessary

Serve with crusty bread

> **Top Tip.**
> The tender raw celery heart is a tasty treat.

Footnote.
When searing taro, do not brown too much as it gets bitter.

Γεμιστά

Bounty Filled Vegetables

Γεμιστά

A Greek cook book would not be complete if certain recipes were not included. Filled vegetables is one of the classics which are synonymous with Greek cuisine. They are referred to as 'Yemista', which simply means 'filled'. The ever-inventive cooks of old devised spectacular ways to invent diverse recipes for vegetables, not only making them taste good, but also making them the 'star' of the meal. This is a skill passed down through the from those who endured poverty and fervently practised periods of fasting. This happened during the times of Lent. Since a hungry Cypriot is not a happy one, this prototypal recipe has passed the test of time and never dates. Many Greek households have their own favoured recipe, and you should too adapt it, as I have, until you are happy with the results. There is a long list of ingredients, as this is normally a celebratory or Sunday dinner, but there in no need to wait until Sunday. Prepare in advance and 'kalin orexi'.

   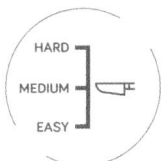  

Preparing the Vegetables

Vegetables

- 2 Large chunky courgettes
- 4 Small red peppers
- 2 Beef tomatoes
- 2 Large potatoes

Filling

- 300g Long grain rice. Rinse and drain in a sieve
- 250g Closed cup mushrooms
- 2 Large onions. Peel and finely chop
- ½ Cup light olive oil
- 30g Flat leaf parsley. Rinse, drain, and finely chop - including the stalks
- 400g Tinned chopped tomatoes
- 2 Tbsp dried mint
- 1 Tsp dried oregano
- 2 Tsp dried cinnamon
- 15g Fresh dill. Rinse, drain, and finely chop. Alternatively, used 2 tsp dried dill

- 1 Tsp tomato purée
- 1 Vegetable/Vegan stock cube dissolved in 1 pint of water
- 1-2 Large lemons, juiced. Use the grated rind of one of them (unwaxed)
- Salt and freshly ground pepper

Cooking Method

Have a large deep ovenproof dish to hand.

Prepare vegetables

1. Discard top and bottom stalk of courgette. Cut in half crosswise and hollow out the middle from the part of courgette that is exposed. Save the flesh in a small bowl, using a knife or small spoon. Do not pierce skin or through to stalk ends
2. Take a small sharp-pointed knife and pierce the top of each of the beef tomatoes in turn. Do this close to the core and rotate until you have cut around, and released, the core. Discard. Now take small spoon and scoop out the flesh and seeds into a bowl and save. Again, try to keep the skin and shape of vegetable intact
3. Peel, rinse, and cut each of the potatoes into quarters lengthwise. Immerse in a bowl of cold water and save to one side
4. Heat a small amount of light olive oil in a medium saucepan and sear the outside of the courgettes, turning them a couple of times. Take out of pan and put to one side to cool

Prepare filling of stuffed yemista

Preheat fan oven to 180-190 degrees C

1. Immerse mushrooms in a bowl of cold water to dislodge any soil, and then put in a colander to drain. Trim ends of stalks, halve, and roughly chop all the mushrooms. Save in a bowl
2. Add the remaining light olive oil to the pan, in which you seared the courgettes. Place on a medium heat, add the finely-chopped onions, and sauté for 2-3 minutes until soft and beginning to colour
3. Stir the mushrooms into the pan and cook for 3-4 minutes
4. Stir the saved courgette flesh into the pan of mushrooms
5. Roughly chop the flesh of the tomatoes you saved earlier, add them any juices and seeds to the pan

6. Add the tomato pasatta and purée, ground mint, oregano, cinnamon and cook out for one minute, turn off heat
7. Stir in the rice, fresh parsley, dill, lemon zest. Add salt, freshly ground pepper and lemon juice to taste
8. Measure water into a jug and dissolve the stock cube. Pour ½ of the stock into the pan and stir. Taste the mixture and adjust the seasoning
9. Using a small spoon stuff all the prepared vegetables nearly to the top, place standing up with the filling facing upwards in the ovenproof pan using all the potatoes to prop them up or fill any gaps. When you have filled all your vegetables go back and fill them to the brim if you have any filling left. Add any remaining potatoes to the dish
10. Pour the remaining stock into the empty pan of filling to deglaze it and then pour the liquid into the bottom of your ovenproof dish. Cover with foil (shiny side down) and bake in a medium oven until the vegetables are completely tender and squatting in the dish, the rice should be soft and the liquid will largely have been absorbed. Divide any juices left in the bottom of pan on top of your vegetables. You may think they do not look presentable when they are well cooked but I promise you they will deliver in taste

Serve with Greek salad, olives, dips and crusty bread.

Top Tip.
There may seem to be a lot of liquid but the rice will absorb most of it.

Footnote.
I always prepare these in advance and bake them a couple of hours before I need to serve. Keep them in a fridge until you are ready to cook them.

Τσίλι κον
Καρνέ
Νηστίσιμο

Chilli Non Carne

Τσίλι κον Καρνέ Νηστίσιμο

The flavours from neighbours in the Mediterranean have really filtered through to Cypriots. The chilli spices and aromatics such as cumin and paprika, have become to many of us firm favourites. Add to those our beloved tomatoes, garlic and onions and behold a dish not too far from our own cuisine. Although we are led to believe chilli con carne as originally a Mexican/American dish, the immigrant Greek restaurateurs that moved to America in the 1920s offered chilli in their restaurants as a zesty and spicy continuation of the Greek cooking style. 'Con carne' means 'with meat', so I have have named this recipe 'non carne' for obvious reasons.

   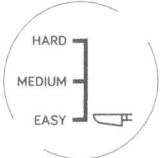  

Preparing the Chilli

- 400g Meat-free mince to suit your preference.
- 2 Onions. Peel and finely chop
- 2 Tbsp light olive oil or a neutral cooking oil
- 4 Cloves garlic. Peel and mince
- 2 Fresh Chillies. Finely chopped. Discard seeds if you do not like a lot of chilli heat
- 200g Chopped tomatoes or overripe fresh tomatoes. Remove skin and core
- 1 Tbsp tomato purée
- 500g Tomato passata
- 3 Tsp ground coriander
- 1-2 Tsp chilli flakes, depending on how spicy you like it
- 2 Tsp ground cumin
- 1 Tsp dried paprika
- Salt and freshly ground pepper to taste
- 1 Vegetable/Vegan stock cube, dissolved in 150ml of water
- 400g Red kidney beans. Tinned and ready to use. Rinse under cold water and drain

Cooking Method

1. Pre-heat pan and oil. Cook onions until light brown and soft
2. Stir in the chilli and spices and cook until you can smell the aromas being released from the spices. Stir in the garlic, being careful not to burn it, as it will become bitter
3. Add the meat-free mince and cook until it browns a little
4. Stir in kidney beans, chopped tomatoes, passata, tomato purée, stock, salt and pepper. Stir and leave to simmer on a medium heat for 25 minutes or until the ingredients have combined and melded. Stir a couple of times
5. Check the liquid and seasonings. Adjust according to taste and serve

Footnote.
If you are using a frozen meat-free product that requires defrosting before cooking, make sure it is thoroughly defrosted before using.

Top Tip.
Check the cooking instructions of the meat-free substitute, as you may need to adapt this recipe accordingly.

Ζυμαρικά

Pasta

Speedy Tomato and Basil Pasta

Σπαγγέτι με Βασιλικό

It is difficult to establish where pasta actually originates from. Popular belief is that it comes from Italy. However, each country has a unique and original type of pasta, and it is more likely to have started life in Ancient Greece called 'Laganon', as it is called, or in some regions as Hilopites. Later records find a form of pasta in China - in the shape of noodles - which were discovered by Marco Polo and taken by him to Italy around the 13th Century. Thereafter, many countries developed their own variation of pasta, such as 'pierogi' in Poland, 'spatzle' in Hungary, and 'orzo' in Greece. The fact is that we all need a speedy, homemade pasta recipe in our reserves for when we neither have the time nor the inclination to shop or cook. This recipe takes less time to cook than a takeaway would to arrive, and is far healthier and nutritious. The use of a few well-selected dried herbs and store-cupboard ingredients replaces the need for a jar of shop-bought pasta sauce, it also has 95% less sugar and salt than a jar of shop bought pasta sauce and little or no preservatives or additives.

  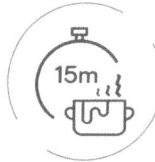 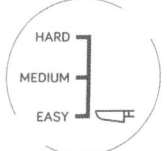 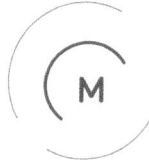 

Preparing the Pasta

- 500g Dried pasta of your choice
- 1 Vegan/vegetarian stock cube
- 300g Chopped tinned tomatoes or tomato pasatta
- 50g Fresh basil, rinsed. Alternatively, 1 heaped tbsp dried basil
- 1 Garlic clove. Peel and mince
- 3 Tbsp light olive oil
- 1 Small cup pasta broth (the cooking liquid from the cooked pasta)
- Salt and pepper to taste

Garnish
- 80g Grated halloumi, parmesan, or vegan alternative

Cooking Method

1. Boil kettle
2. Heat the oil in a medium-sized saucepan on a low heat. Stir in the garlic quickly followed by the tomatoes and basil. Gently simmer
3. Cook pasta in boiling stock, season with salt, and cook for 2 minutes less than the instructions on the packet
4. When your pasta is ready, drain it and pour it into the tomato sauce. Stir in some of the broth you retained until you are happy with the consistency of the sauce. Cook for a further 1-2 minutes until pasta absorbs some of the liquid. Add the pepper. Taste and adjust seasoning if necessary
5. Turn off heat and stir in half of the grated cheese. Divide the pasta into serving bowls, sprinkle the remaining cheese equally between them, and serve

Easy momemade pizza

Follow from step 2 of the above recipe. Add 1 tsp of tomato purée, salt and pepper to taste. Simmer the sauce until it reduces in volume by 1/3. Use it as the tomato base for pizzas. You can buy plain pizza bases or any flatbread you prefer and top them with whatever you choose. This is a far healthier, quicker and cheaper than shop bought. It's also a great way to encourage children to cook and eat.

Top Tip.
You can adapt this basic recipe any way you like. For example, you add chilli flakes for spice, replace tinned tomatoes with fresh cherry tomatoes, wilt rinsed spinach along with the pasta just before you drain it, or simply add mushrooms, courgettes, or peppers at step 2.

Σοφή σάλτσα
Ζυμαρικών

Wise Owl Pasta Sauce

Σοφή σάλτσα Ζυμαρικών

Greeks often have a familial nickname which stems from days of old, which was a method they used to differentiate families. Surnames would often be quoted, along with a nickname, derived from one's birth town or village, profession, trade, or even an unusual or extreme external appearance. This brings me to the name of this appetising pasta sauce, adopted from a great, great grandfather, and befitting a recipe which camouflages vegetables in a manner that your vegetable decliners will not recognise. I will leave it up to your imagination as to how the family acquired the 'owl' nickname! This is a low sugar, low salt, vegetable-laden pasta sauce for an easy, nutritious everyday meal.

  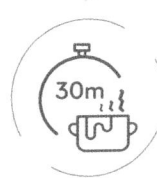 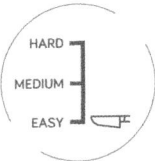 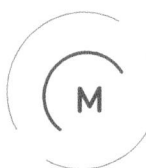 

Preparing the Sauce

- 500g Dry pasta of your choice
- 1 Courgette. Discard top and bottom stalks and rinse
- 1 Carrot. Discard top and bottom stalk, peel and rinse
- 2 Celery stalks. Trim and discard top and bottom stalks, rinse, and discard any fibrous string
- 1 Onion. Peeled
- 200g Mushrooms. Quickly submerse mushrooms in cold water and drain in a colander
- 1 Pepper. Red, yellow or orange. Discard seeds and pith
- 2 Garlic cloves. Peel and mince
- 400g Tomato pasatta or tinned chopped tomatoes
- 1 Tbsp tomato purée
- 1 Tsp ground cinnamon
- 1 Tsp ground dry mint
- 1 Tsp oregano or thyme
- 4 Tbsp light olive oil
- 1 Vegetable stock cube suitable for vegans.
- 1 Bay leaf
- 100ml Dry fruity red wine (optional)
- Salt (optional)
- Freshly ground pepper to taste
- 1 Small cup pasta broth (reserve from the cooking pasta)

Garnish
- 80g Grated halloumi or hard vegan cheese alternative

Cooking Method

1. Grate the onion, carrot, and courgette on the large side of a box grater
2. Cut celery in half crosswise, in 4 lengthwise, then finely dice
3. Heat the oil in a large-sized saucepan on a medium heat and then stir the grated onions into the pan. Cook until the onions are soft and beginning to take on colour
4. Add the remaining grated vegetables and the diced celery to the onions. Sauté for 3-4 minutes or until they begin to soften, stirring regularly
5. Trim stalks of mushrooms, cut into small dice, and then add them to the pan
6. Stir in the garlic, cinnamon, mint, oregano, tomato purée, and red wine. Cook for 2-3 minutes to cook out the alcohol
7. Chop peppers into dice and add to the pan
8. Boil kettle and cook pasta in boiling, salted stock for 2 minutes less than the instructions on the packet advise
9. Add the tomato pasatta, bay leaf, and some of the reserved pasta liquid to the vegetables
10. Cook on a low simmer for 15 minutes or until the liquid has reduced a little in volume and developed a darker more uniform colour
11. Drain pasta (reserve 1 small cup of liquid). Stir into the sauce and cook for 1-2 minutes. Add some of the reserved stock if it is not cooked to your liking and, continue to cook a little while longer. Taste and adjust seasoning if necessary

Serve with the grated cheese in a serving bowl and allow your diners to sprinkle to taste.

Footnote.
Use a wholewheat pasta or a 50/50 pasta mix, which is 50% durum wheat and 50% wholewheat. This does not differ a great deal in flavour but is far better nutritionally.

> **Top Tip.**
> Double up this recipe for the sauce and, freeze leftovers in an airtight container with a lid.

Κριθαράκι

Opulent Orzo & Mushroom Pasta

Κριθαράκι

Orzo is a short-cut pasta, shaped like rice. We Cypriots call it 'kritharaki', which means 'little barley'. Orzo pasta is quick, simple, and delicious and is widely used in Mediterranean and Middle Eastern cuisine. Like pasta, it is a great vehicle for flavour. With just 4 humble ingredients, you will have a dish that your family and friends will love and that is a great accompaniment to just about anything. I will never forget the first time I cooked this pasta. Under the impression that it should be prepared like rice, I went on to rinse it, and the result was a sticky mess which lumped together. Needless to say, do not rinse orzo.

   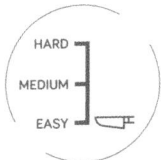  

Preparing the Pasta

- 500g Orzo pasta
- 1 Large onion. Peel and finely chop
- 300g Tomato pasatta
- 300g Closed cup mushrooms (white or chestnut). Cut into quarters (optional)
- 4-5 Tbsp light olive oil
- 1 Tbsp tomato purée
- 1 Vegetable/vegan stock cube, dissolved
- 1 Tsp dried cinammon (optional)
- 1.5 Litres hot water
- Salt and freshly ground pepper to taste

Garnish
- Grated halloumi as much you like, or a vegan hard cheese alternative. Parmesan works well too

Cooking Method

1. Boil kettle
2. Heat a saucepan on a medium heat and add most of the oil. Stir in the onions and sauté until they are soft and taking on a light golden colour
3. Add the remaining oil to another pan. Then stir in the mushrooms and sauté on medium-high heat until they are tender and taking on a little colour. Season with salt to taste. When cooked, take off the heat
4. Measure the hot water in a jug and dissolve the stock cube
5. Add the orzo to the pan of onions. Stir well until evenly coated with oil. Place pan on the smallest ring on your hob and on to the lowest heat. Then stir in the tomato pasatta and cook for a minute or two
6. Pour in the stock and stir using a wooden spoon. Add salt and freshly ground pepper to taste
7. Continue to stir gently and regularly until the liquid has nearly all been absorbed. Stir in the cooked mushrooms and taste. Add a little more water if the orzo is not soft to bite. Add more seasoning if required
8. When you are happy with the texture of the orzo turn off heat and serve. You are looking for a fluid texture such as a risotto

Serve with grilled halloumi or crumbled feta cheese (or vegan substitutes) and a dressed salad.

Footnote.
Add rinsed and drained spinach at Step 6 to make this a one-pot dish that simply requires a garnish of grated halloumi or feta cheese. If using mushrooms, ensure they are of the closed cup variety, as the black gills of open cup types will leak into your finished dish, ruining the fresh vibrant colour.

Top Tip.
Keep stirring on a low heat. Orzo sticks very easily to the bottom of the pan.

Σαλάτα με
Φούσιλι

Family Favourite Fusilli Salad

Σαλάτα με Φούσιλι

Everything about this dish lends itself to being a perfect family meal - whatever the weather! The fusilli pasta, black olives, and cherry tomatoes make this dish look really inviting, if deceptively complex. Yet, it is so easy to make. I serve this at baby showers, garden parties, picnics and family meals. Any leftovers go in a lunchbox for school or work. Although this dish tasted especially good on holiday under the canopy of the vine trees, the back garden or local park with friends or family must suffice. I like to eat this chilled, but if you prefer to eat as soon as it's prepared, go ahead.

Preparing the Salad

- 500g Fusili pasta
- 225g Spinach. Rinse and drain
- 250g Cherry tomatoes. Rinse and halve
- 100g Black kalamata olives (pitted)
- 200g Greek feta cheese or vegan alternative. Cube
- 3 Tbsp extra virgin olive oil
- ½ Red onion. Peel and finely slice
- 1 Lemon, juiced
- 1 Vegan/vegetarian stock cube
- Salt and freshly ground pepper to taste

Cooking Method

1. Dissolve stock in a saucepan of hot water. Season with salt, and stir in the pasta. Boil pasta for 2 minutes less than on the instructions. Then, when the pasta is nearly cooked, stir in the spinach and cook until the spinach wilts. Reserve ½ cup of stock and leave to one side. Drain the pasta in a colander

2. Pour the cooked and drained pasta into a large airtight container with a lid. Add 2 Tbsp of extra virgin olive oil and put the lid on. Shake gently to coat the pasta in oil, take lid off, and allow to cool

3. Add the olives, tomatoes, pepper, onion, ½ the lemon juice, and 1-2 tbsp of the reserved stock. Put the lid on and shake gently to mix, or use a spatula

4. Taste and add more lemon juice, olive oil, salt and pepper if necessary. If the pasta is sticking, add some of the reserved stock - one spoonful at a time. Add the feta or alternative, mix in gently, cover with lid, and refrigerate

Footnote.
Swap or add tinned sweetcorn, peas, broccoli florets.

Top Tip.
Make in advance, as it keeps well in the fridge.

Ζυμαρικά με κολοκύθι και καυτερή πιπεριά

Spicy Courgette Pasta

Ζυμαρικά με κολοκύδι και καυτερή πιπεριά

Some people bring souvenirs back from their holidays. I do too, but they are invariably of the edible or potable variety. I love getting home and stretching my holiday experience with a home-cooked meal, enhanced with an ingredient or two that came home in my suitcase. My dearly departed father would always pick 3-4 ripe lemons from a tree in his orchard for me to bring home. On one occasion, this dish was inspired by a marrow - 'Κολοκύθι' (large courgette), which had travelled home with the lemons - and this dish was created. Although Cypriot lemons have an unparalleled aroma and flavour, this quick and delicious dish is reminiscent of those flavours.

  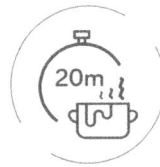 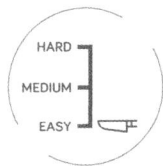  

Preparing the Pasta

- 2 Large courgettes. Rinse and dry. Discard top and bottom stalks. Then, grate on large side of box grater onto a plate. Leave to one side

or

- 1 Marrow (discard seeds and soft centre). Prepare in the same way as the courgette

and

- 500g Spaghetti or linguine (or any type of pasta you have in your store cupboard)
- 1 Tbsp tomato purée
- 1 Large onion. Peel and finely chop
- 4 Tbsp light olive oil
- 1-2 Lemons (unwaxed). Juice and zest and discard pips
- 1 Clove garlic. Peel and mince
- 1 Vegetable stock cube suitable for vegans
- 1 Tbsp dried chilli flakes or more to taste
- 100g Grated aged halloumi, or any hard cheese of your choice, or vegan alternative (optional)
- Salt and freshly ground pepper to taste

Cooking Method

1. Add the pasta to a saucepan of salted boiling water, in which you have dissolved the stock cube. Boil the pasta for two minutes less than the instructions advse. Drain in a colander, reserving 1 cup of the cooking stock. Pour the pasta back into the pan

2. Whilst the pasta is cooking, heat a frying pan on a medium heat. Add the oil and stir in the onions. Season with salt, so as to help prevent them browning whilst cooking. Cook until very soft, but still translucent. Do not colour the onions

3. Stir in the garlic, and quickly add the grated courgettes, so that the garlic does not burn and become bitter

4. Sauté for 3-4 minutes, then add the tomato purée. Continue to cook for 2-3 minutes, then add to the pan of cooked, drained pasta

5. Turn heat down to low, whilst you stir in the lemon juice, zest, chilli flakes, salt, pepper, and half of the stock

6. Taste and adjust seasoning if necessary. When the pasta is cooked to your liking, stir in the grated cheese. Otherwise add the remaining stock and cook on low heat for a further 1-2 minutes, before adding the cheese

Serve with broccoli or green beans, and toasted crusty bread scraped with a peeled garlic clove and a brush of extra virgin olive oil.

> **Top Tip.**
> Add a little of the stock from the pasta to the pan, in which you are cooking the broccoli or green beans. Simply pan fry with light olive oil and garlic for a minute or two. Then, add stock to soften and flavour the vegetables. When they are cooked, season with a little squeeze of lemon juice, and serve.

Παστίτσιο

Legendary Layered Pastichio Pasta

Παστίτσιο

This is my 'go-to' dish when I am cooking for a large number of people. As this recipe is super flexible, I can adapt it according to my guests' dietary requirements. It can be made in advance, eaten warm, cold, or reheated. Perhaps because of all the above, and, not least due to its delicious, greeklicious taste, it is a traditional, timeless classic, which I have brought bang up to date with great substitutes and alternative ingredients. The mainland Greeks call this dish 'pastichio'. Us Cypriots call it 'makaronia tou fournou', 'pasta baked in the oven'. There is no disguising the extra effort required in preparing this layered pasta dish. All I can say is when you try this soft, creamy, flavourful dish, you will make it again and again, and your guests will not realise that it is a vegetarian dish - let alone vegan!

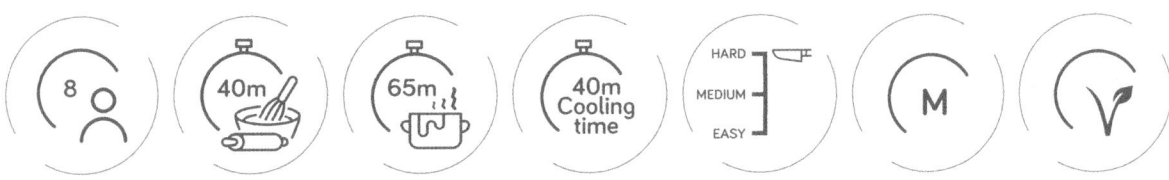

Preparing the Pasta

You will need a deep ovenproof dish 10"x12"x3" deep

Pasta layer

- 500g Long mezzani macaroni pasta, A or B width, or pasta bucatini, rigatoni, paccheri, tortiglioni, or ziti
- 40g Grated aged halloumi (see notes in ingredients section if you are not sure which cheese to use instead of aged halloumi) or a vegan hard cheese alternative
- 1 Vegan/vegetarian stock cube
- ½ Tsp ground mint (combine with the grated halloumi)
- Salt to taste

Vegetable layer

- 500-600g Mixed vegetables - any combination from frozen or tinned sweetcorn, chopped fresh closed cup mushrooms, fresh peppers, courgettes, aubergines, fresh blanched green beans and wilted, drained, chopped fresh spinach. Rinse, dry, drain and discard top and bottom stalks, pith and seeds accordingly. Then, chop all vegetables to roughly the same size pieces - like large dice
- 2 Large onions. Peel and roughly chop
- 3-4 Large ripe tomatoes. Discard skins and cores (to skin a tomato, score an x in the bottom of tomato through to the skin and place in boiling water until the skin starts to peel away. Then, peel off with a knife). Chop the tomatoes into large dice-sized pieces and save to one side including the seeds and juice

- 100g Tomato passata
- 1 Tbsp tomato purée
- 4 Tbsp light olive oil
- 30g Flat leaf parsley. Rinse, dry and trim stalks, but retain the rest and roughly chop
- 1 Tbsp dried ground mint
- 1 Tsp dried oregano
- 1 Tsp dried cinnamon
- Salt and freshly ground pepper to taste

Béchamel sauce layer

- 1.3 Litres fresh milk (or oat or almond milk work well as the vegan substitutes)
- 100ml Pasta cooking liquor
- 150g Plain flour
- 150g Light olive oil or a neutral cooking oil
- 1 Large egg, beaten (omit if you're vegan)
- 230g Grated aged halloumi or a vegan hard cheese alternative
- Salt and pepper to taste

Cooking Method

Assembling the dish

1. Begin by cooking the pasta in a large pan of salted boiling water with the stock cube. Boil until it is 'al dente'. Do not cook until soft. Drain the pasta, but retain 2 cups of the cooking stock. Pour pasta into the ovenproof dish. Add 1/2 of the retained pasta stock to the dish and shake to coat the base

2. Use the cheese allocated to the pasta layer and sprinkle it over evenly. Flatten pasta with the back of a large spoon or a spatula and ensure it is as even as possible and goes right into corners and sides of the dish

3. For the vegetable layer, heat a saucepan on a medium to high heat. Add the oil, and when it is hot, add the onions, cook until soft and beginning to colour. Then, stir in the chopped tomatoes and cook for a minute

4. Stir in all the dried herbs, spices, tomato purée and tomato passata. If you are using spinach, stir that in too, so as to draw out all of its moisture

5. Add all the remaining vegetables and fresh parsley into the onions and cook for 2-3 minutes. Pour in the remaining stock, season with salt and pepper, and gently simmer for 8-10 minutes. Taste and adjust the seasoning if necessary. You are looking for quite a fluid mixture. Turn off heat. Spoon the vegetable layer over the pasta as evenly as possible, taking the vegetables into the corners and sides. Take care to cover the pasta completely. Flatten and press down firmly with a spoon or a spatula so that you have an even surface. Leave to one side

For the Béchamel sauce layer

1. Have all the utensils and ingredients to hand, including a balloon hand whisk, a spatula, and all the measured ingredients. Preheat fan oven 180-190 degrees C

2. Add the oil to a saucepan. Put on a medium heat and whisk in the flour until you have a smooth paste. Cook for 2-3 minutes

3. Whisk in the milk, stirring constantly, whilst gently simmering, until the sauce thickens. Take care to go round the sides of the pan with the whisk too. When the sauce has thickened and begun to bubble, turn down heat to the lowest possible. Whisk in 200g of the grated halloumi allocated to the bechamel sauce. Add salt and pepper to taste. Add some of the pasta cooking liquor, a little at a time, if the sauce becomes very thick. If you are adding egg, then take the pan off the heat and whisk it in quickly. Check seasoning and adjust

4. Pour the sauce evenly over the vegetables, taking care to completely cover the surface of the dish and go right into corners and sides. Give the dish a little tap on the counter top to help it settle, and make room for the sauce. Sprinkle the remaining grated halloumi evenly over the surface of the bechamel. Let it set for 15 minutes before you bake in the oven

5. Place in the oven and check after 45 minutes to ensure it is browning evenly all over. If not, rotate dish, and continue to bake until it is evenly golden brown all over

6. Let it cool for at least 60 minutes before you cut, so that it is firm enough to serve.

Serve with a Greek salad, 'Not Kleftico', or rosemary and garlic potatoes.

Top Tip.
Make a few hours in advance and bake 2-3 hrs before you need to serve. Pastichio firms as it cools, which enables neater and visually-pleasing portions - especially good for large gatherings.

Footnote.
Taste all the layers as you go along, and before you assemble the dish, especially as the vegan cheeses vary in flavour. Once assembled, it will be impossible to adjust the seasoning.

Rice

Τρίχρωμο Ρύζι της Γιαγιάς

Irene's Tricolour Rice

Τρίχρωμο Ρύζι τις Γιαγιάς

Years ago, in the early 1960s, my late mother came to the UK. She had a lucky encounter at a bus stop with a Greek lady, who had lived in the UK for a number of years. That lady was called Irene and she took my mother under her wing. She was often at our home when my siblings and I got home from school, and we would regularly be greeted with something delicious as well as a warm hug. 'Yiayia' Irene had a beautiful presence and, with patience, she taught me how to prepare many dishes. This quick, healthy, and adaptable rice pilaf was one of them. She also taught me how to make a proper cup of tea. It should be brewed on the hob, under a very low heat, with 1 teabag per person, 1 whole spice clove, and a small piece of cassia bark. Back to the rice. It has remained a dish that we make at least once a week in some form or other. It goes well on its own or with pretty much anything. This easy rice dish is an inter-generational recipe loved by children and adults alike, and is a simple dish that you can teach children to prepare themselves.

   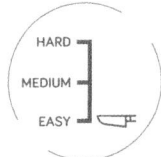  

Preparing the Rice

- 1 Large onion. Peel and finely chop
- 300g Rinsed long grain rice, drained
- 160-200g Closed cup white or chestnut mushrooms. Rinse, trim and discard stalks. Cut into slices or quarters
- 160g Tinned or frozen sweetcorn. Defrost before adding to recipe
- 80g Frozen peas or petit pois
- 70ml Light olive oil
- 600ml Hot water
- 1 Large knob of butter, margarine or vegan alternative
- 1 Vegetable stock cube suitable for vegans. Dissolve in 100ml of warm water

Cooking Method

1. Boil kettle
2. Add the light olive oil to a preheated medium-sized saucepan
3. Stir in the onions and sauté until soft and evenly golden brown
4. In a separate pan, melt the margarine, and then add the chopped mushrooms. Cook on a high heat until they become tender and are lightly browned
5. Add the drained rice to the pan and stir well to completely coat all the grains in oil. This seals the rice and prevents the grains sticking together
6. Turn down heat to low and add the hot water, stock, salt and pepper, stir then push any rice grains that may be stuck on sides of the pan under the water
7. Simmer gently for 10 minutes then stir in the mushrooms, frozen peas, and sweetcorn, and simmer for a further 2-3 minutes or until the liquid has been absorbed. Turn off heat, cover with a lid, and allow the rice to rest for a few minutes before serving

Serve with a dressed salad and plain greek yogurt.

Footnote.
Rice does not keep well. Eat on the same day that it is cooked.

Top Tip.
You can add or remove the vegetables as you please, and make a simple rice dish without them.

Ρύση με
Φιδέ Πιλάφι

Bronzed Vermicelli Pilaf

Ρύση με Φιδέ Πιλάφι

'Vermicelli' is a variety of pasta that is almost as fine as threads of cotton. It can be purchased cut or whole. When whole, it resembles fine, delicate birds nests. 'Pilaf' simply means 'cooked together with rice'. This is another dish, for which many countries have a version. The technique of charring the pasta is something we Cypriots share cheifly with Middle Eastern countries. It adds a very unique flavour and texture to the rice, which gives it that hint of something exotic and special, even though it is an everyday day recipe that is very simple to prepare and a pleasing accompaniment to many other dishes. This is yet another family staple that you will prepare and enjoy on a regular basis.

   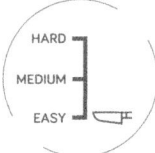  

Preparing the Pilaf

- 320g Long grain rice. Rinse well and pour into a sieve to drain.
- 1 Large onion. Peel and finely chop
- 80-100g Cut vermicelli (if whole, simply place a nest or two into a small food bag and crush with your fist)
- 4 Tbsp light olive oil or any neutral cooking oil
- 1 Vegetable/vegan stock cube (dissolved)
- Salt and pepper to taste
- 640ml Hot water

Cooking Method

1. Boil kettle
2. Pour rinsed rice into a measuring jug. Note the level it comes to and times by 2 for the amount of water you need, or use the measurements I have provided. Put rice into a sieve to drain and pour the amount of water you require from the kettle into the jug, and stir in the stock cube until it dissolves
3. Heat a pan and add the oil. Put on a medium to high heat and add the onions and vermicelli. Fry for 3-5 minutes or until the vermicelli is dark bronze colour - almost charred. Stir often
4. Pour the rice into the pan and stir well, so as to coat the grains of rice in the oil. This seals the grains and prevents them sticking together
5. Add the stock, salt to taste, and stir. Push all the grains of rice into the liquid. Turn down heat to low and simmer rice for 10-12 minutes. Stir once, halfway through the cooking time
6. When the rice has little holes bubbling on the surface, it is ready to switch off. Do not let it boil dry. Switch off heat and cover with a lid. Let the dish stand for a few minutes so that any moisture is absorbed using the residual heat of the pan. Use a fork to fluff rice before serving

Serve with Greek yoghurt, Mouthwatering Malt Mushrooms, Greek salad, feta salad, and/or any of the roasted vegetable recipes. The list is endless.

Top Tip.
Do not boil rice on too high a heat. It will absorb liquid too quickly and still be chalky in the centre. Also, do not stir too often, as you will have sticky rice.

Footnote.
Do not worry about getting too dark a colour on the vermicelli, as it pales during the cooking stage when water is added.

Πικάντικο
Ρύζι

Nice 'n' Spicy Rice

Πικάντικο Ρύζι

My family's love of spice has infiltrated some of my recipes. We also love rice and the two have naturally fused together. The main ingredients are not too far removed from authentic Greek rice dishes, albeit tweaked a little with embezzled spices from our Middle Eastern neighbours. This dish hits the mark when I need a quick, tasty one-pot dish. It bakes in the oven, whilst I potter about -no fuss; little mess; and great results!

   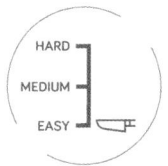  

Preparing the Rice

A sauté pan or any ovenproof deep frying pan, with a lid, is best for this dish.

- 300g Long grain rice. Rinse and drain in a sieve
- ½ Whole celery. Separate stalks and choose some with the leaves. Rinse, cut in four lengthwise, chop into small dice, and place in a bowl to one side
- 1 Large onion. Peel and finely chop
- 1 Large garlic clove, minced
- 1 Red pepper. Rinse, cut into thin strips and finely dice
- 150g Garden peas or petit pois
- 350g Tomato pasatta
- 1 Fresh red chilli, finely sliced. Add more and leave seeds in if you like it really spicy
- 50ml Light olive oil
- 1 Tsp ground cinnamon
- 1 Tsp chilli flakes
- 1 Tsp celery salt
- 1 Tsp garlic granules
- 1 Vegan/vegetarian stock cube, dissolved
- 675ml Hot water
- Salt and pepper to taste

Cooking Method

1. Preheat oven to medium - 210-220 degrees C
2. Boil kettle
3. Heat the frying pan on a medium heat on the cooker top. Heat the oil and stir in the onions. Sauté until golden brown
4. Measure the hot water from the kettle and dissolve the stock cube in it. Turn down heat to low
5. Stir in the celery, minced garlic, dried herbs, and spices
6. Stir in the rice until it is all coated with oil
7. Stir in the tomato pasatta
8. Pour in the stock and the diced pepper, stir well with a wooden spoon to evenly distribute ingredients
9. Season sparingly with salt and pepper, as this dish is heavily spiced and the celery salt contains salt
10. Place in the oven with the lid on and bake for 25 minute. Then add the frozen peas and push them into the rice with a fork.
11. Put back in the oven for 5 minutes with the lid on

Serve with cooling tsatsiki or talatouri and a feta salad or a spoonful of Greek yogurt or vegan alternatives.

> **Top Tip.**
> Take care not to rub your eyes if you do not wear gloves whilst handling the fresh chillies.

Ρύζι πιλάφι

Surreptitious Speckled Pilaf

Ρύζι πιλάφι

Getting vegetables in a diet - especially that of children, is challenging. Reaching the ever-changing guidelines on a daily basis is difficult enough. Doing it in style is another matter altogether! I developed this covert vegetable-and-rice dish organically, which nourished my children when they where little - and they never once cottoned on that it was packed full of vegetables. It is a life saver for those who need a break from the screams of "I don't like it!", when they produce vegetables for dinner. In true Greek fashion, this dish is tasty, healthy, and quick. It's speckled appearance is created by the cooked hidden vegetables, which gives this dish its name.

   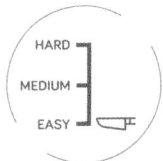  

Preparing the Pilaf

- 300g Long grain rice. Rinse and drain
- 1 Large carrot. Rinse, discard top and bottom stalks and peel. Stand a box grater on a plate and grate on the large side of box grater. Leave the grated carrot to one side
- 1 Large courgette. Rinse and discard top and bottom stalks. Stand box grater on a plate and grate on the large side of box grater. Leave to one side
- 2-3 Celery stalks. Rinse, trim top and bottom of stalks, pull any strings from the celery with your fingers, and discard (if using the outer more fibrous stalks). Cut celery in 4 lengthwise, and then finely dice
- 1 Large onion. Peel and finely chop
- 4 Tbsp light olive oil
- 1 Vegetable stock cube suitable for vegans. Dissolve in 25ml of water
- 650ml Hot water
- Salt and freshly ground pepper to taste

Cooking Method

1. Boil kettle
2. Heat a saucepan on a medium heat and add the oil. When the oil is hot, stir in the onion with a wooden spoon. Sauté the onion for 3-5 minutes or until it begins to colour evenly
3. Stir in all the grated vegetables and sauté for 5-6 minutes and cook until they begin to wilt and release their moisture
4. Turn down heat to low, stir in the rice, and mix until all the grains are coated with oil and glistening
5. Measure the water and pour into the saucepan. Stir until all the ingredients are evenly mixed
6. Add the stock and salt and pepper
7. Simmer gently for 12 minutes, or until little bubbles begin to pop up through the rice and the liquid has been absorbed. Do not stir. You can, however, make a space with a fork to the bottom of the pan to check the liquid if you are in doubt
8. Turn off the heat. Put a lid on and let the rice stand for a few minutes. Fluff the rice with a fork before serving

Serve with any of the following: 'No Meat Tomato Balls', cucumber and carrot sticks, cherry tomatoes, hummus, tahini, greek yoghurt, and olives.

Footnote.
Omit the salt completely if you are feeding young children or weaning toddlers. There is an adequate amount of salt in the stock cube.

Top Tip.
This is a perfect buffet or meze dish, as it goes well with almost everything.

Σπανακόρυσο

Spinach & Rice Pilaf

Σπανακόρυσο

Spinach is another crop that the Cypriots grow in abundance. You will no doubt have heard of the legendary 'spanakopita' or spinach pie. This traditional recipe is a method devised to use the generous yields of spinach or chard from the villagers' allotments or local market, called the 'Agora'. 'Pilaf' is another term for pilau. What seems a huge amount of spinach is simply stirred into the pan, so that it wilts in with the rice. Once more, this is another dish that requires few ingredients and little time and effort, but produces scrumptious yet healthy results.

  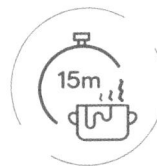 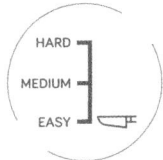  

Preparing the Pilaf

- 320g Long grain rice. Rinse and pour into a sieve to drain
- 200-300g Rinsed and drained spinach
- 1 Large onion. Peel and finely chop
- 300g Tomato pasatta or chopped tinned tomatoes
- 4-5 Tbsp light olive oil
- 1 Vegetable/vegan stock cube, dissolved
- 1 Tsp ground cinnamon (optional)
- Salt to taste
- Lots of freshly ground pepper
- 640ml Hot water

Cooking Method

1. Boil Kettle
2. Heat a saucepan and add the oil, heat on a medium to high heat, stir in the onions, and sauté for 2-3 minutes until soft and translucent
3. Pour the hot water into a jug and dissolve the stock cube into it
4. Stir in the chopped tomatoes/passata and ground cinnamon, and cook for 1-2 minutes
5. Add the rice - stirring well to coat the grains completely in the oil
6. Turn down heat to very low. Add the stock and stir well with a wooden spoon until all the rice is covered by the liquid. Season with salt and pepper and cook for 10 minutes
7. After 10 minutes, stir the spinach into the rice in 3-4 batches, so as to make room for it to wilt into the pan. Cook for a further 5 minutes or until the liquid has been absorbed. Do not allow the pilaf to cook dry. Check the seasoning, and turn off heat. Put the lid on, and let the rice stand for 10 minutes

Serve with a heaped spoonful of Greek yogurt or a drizzle of olive oil, and squeeze of lemon juice.

Top Tip.
Vary the amount of spinach to your taste. My family like heaps of spinach.

Footnote.
The cinnamon elevates this dish and gives it a warm undertone.

Φασόλια
και
Όσπρια

Beans, Pulses & Legumes

Φακόρυζο

Lovable Lentil Stew

Φακόρυζο

We Cypriots call this rice and lentil stew 'Φακές' - 'lentils'. 'μουτζεντρα' – 'moutsendra' simply means 'rice and lentil stew'. I believe the word 'moutsendra' has its origins in Middle Eastern lentil recipes, from which Cypriots inherited the name. Nevertheless, this Cypriot recipe dates back hundreds of years. I use brown lentils, as they do not need to be soaked overnight, and are very tasty. You may not think this recipe sounds very appealing, but do not be discouraged, as it is both delicious and highly nutritious. Generations of Cypriots prepare their own variation of this regularly and with good reason! It is a family pleaser for young and old alike that is packed full of iron and great for expectant mothers. We introduce this dish to our babies as soon as they are old enough to eat solids.

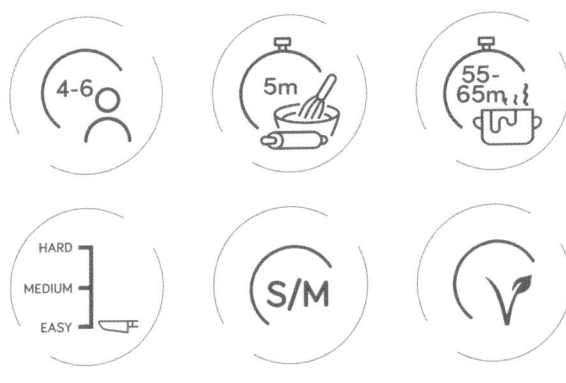

Preparing the Stew

- 500g Brown lentils. Wash well in a bowl of cold water, discard any tiny pebbles or floating lentils and drain well
- 80g Long grain rice. Rinse and leave in a sieve to drain
- 2 Large onions. Peel and finely chopped
- 300g Tomato passata or chopped tomatoes
- 1 Celery stalk. Cut in half crosswise and then in 4 lengthwise. Chop into dice (optional)
- 1 Tbsp tomato purée
- 1 Vegetable stock cube suitable for vegans, dissolved
- 150ml Light olive oil
- 30ml Extra virgin olive oil
- Salt and freshly ground pepper to taste

Cooking Method

1. Put washed lentils in a saucepan and cover them with cold water 2-3" above lentils. Bring to boil and cook for 15 minutes, stirring a couple of times. Boil kettle

2. When the lentils have been cooking for 15 minutes, drain the liquid completely in a large colander. Then, rinse lentils quickly with cold running water. Leave to one side for a moment whilst you rinse the saucepan with cold water to remove any scum from the sides of the pan

3. Heat a smaller saucepan and add both of the oils. Place on a low heat. When hot, add the onions and cook them, stirring every now and then. They need to be golden and caramelised. Therefore, let them cook away slowly and gently whilst the lentils cook

4. Return the lentils to the clean saucepan and cover them again by 3-4" with the hot boiled water from the kettle. You may need to boil the kettle again. Continue to cook lentils for another 20 minutes. Stir occasionally. Check that your onions are not burning

5. After the 20 minutes, try a lentil. If they are soft add the celery, rice, stock cube and salt to taste. If they are not soft, continue to cook before you do this. Cook the lentils with the rice for a further 20 minutes on a medium heat. The mixture should still be quite fluid. If not, add more hot water

6. Stir the tomato pasatta and tomato purée in with the cooked onions, and cook out for one minute. Take 1/2 cup of the lentil stew and place to one side, whilst you add the onions, oil, and everything else to the soft lentils. Pour the cup of reserved lentil stew into the pan, in which you cooked the onions to deglaze the pan. Then add this to the lentil stew. Stir well to mix all the ingredients

7. Continue to cook on a low heat for 5-10 minutes, allowing the flavours to merge, add freshly ground pepper and more salt if required. Turn off heat, cover with a lid, and allow the lentil stew to rest for 5 minutes before serving

Serve with plain Greek yogurt, batons of cucumber, fresh tomatoes, olives, and grilled halloumi. Cypriots traditionally eat lentils with any tinned fish such as mackerel, sardines, or anchovies - if they are not fasting. Alternatively, they have eggs fried in light olive oil.

Top Tip.
Do not be alarmed by the amount of oil in this recipe. It really adds to the flavour of the dish.

Footnote.
Do not burn the onions as they will become bitter.

Λουβία
Μαύρομάτικα

Black-Eyed Bean stew

Λούβια Μαύροματικα

Black-eyed beans are a legume. In the UK, we can easily buy them in packets that require soaking overnight. They are also available in specialist stores when in season as a fresh vegetable/legume. They look like green beans. These pods are shaped like runner beans and have the black-eyed seeds in them. Manufacturers remove and then dry the seeds to give us the black-eyed beans we buy in shops. They are hugely popular with Cypriots, who class this dish as 'the king' of fasting recipes. My passion for food began when I ate this dish. I vividly remember, years ago, as a young girl at my grandparents' home in Cyprus, sat top and tailing the fresh beans, still bearing their seeds. I did this alongside my aunts ready for my grandmother to cook for us. She served them with large courgettes, known as 'marrows' (same family as courgettes and cucumber -peculiarly they are all classed as fruit), and greens or chard – 'lahana'. They were then laced with a copious amount of extra virgin olive oil and freshly-squeezed lemon juice. Lemons are another fruit grown in Cyprus, which taste out if this world. I cook this dish regularly and it has long been one of my own family's favourite dishes.

Soaking Time Overnight

   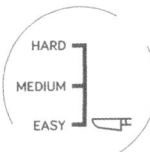 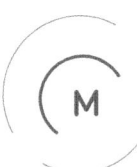 

Preparing the Stew

- 500g Black-eyed beans. Soak overnight. (Do not confuse with black turtle beans)
- 1 Large marrow or 2-3 large courgettes. Rinse, discard top and bottom stalks, and cut into 8 pieces
- 500g Chard or spring greens. Wash in a bowl of cold water, cut off and discard the end of stalks, slice into large pieces, and put in a colander to drain
- Salt to taste
- Crusty bread to serve (optional)

Dressing

- ½-1 Cup extra virgin olive oil
- 2-3 Lemons, cut into halves
- Table or sea salt (optional)

> **Top Tip.**
> To make chopping the greens easier, roll a few pieces at a time into a cigar shape, and then chop. Garnish the finished serving of black-eyed bean stew generously with oil and lemon, which will enhance both the taste and appearance,. Pour it on and stir it in.

Footnote.
Do not be discouraged by the darkness of the broth. Black-eyed beans are nutrient dense, and high in iron, thiamine, and protein. The broth holds a lot of those benefits. Do not drain away the goodness. The bread is optional, although I included it on the ingredients list, as it is a 'must' to have some to mop up all the juices. You can also add peeled potatoes, which you have cut in half at Step 8, if you like.

Cooking Method

1. Boil kettle
2. Drain the soaking liquid from the black-eyed beans
3. Pour into a saucepan and cover generously with the boiled water. Boil until a volcano of scum begins to erupt. Drain, rinse the pan clean, and wipe the sides with a clean damp cloth if necessary. Cover generously with water and continue to boil
4. Cook on a high heat for at least 10 minutes or until a volcano of froth begins to rise. Then, boil the kettle again whilst you drain the beans. Then, put them back on to cook for a further 30 minutes with freshly boiled water. Clean the inside of the pan if any scum is stuck to the sides
5. Repeat step 4 and continue to boil the beans for another 30 minutes
6. During cooking, skim off any scum from the surface of the beans with a large spoon and add more water if the beans are not completely covered
7. If the beans are not soft, continue to cook on a medium heat for 15 minutes. Stir a couple of times
8. Stir in the marrow and add salt to taste. Continue to cook on a medium heat for 15 minutes
9. Add the chard/greens and use a spoon to push them into the broth. Do not crush the delicate marrows, give the pan a gentle shake from side to side, and ensure the level of liquid covers 1/3 of the vegetables. Continue to cook for a further 25 minutes or until the beans and vegetables are very soft and dark green in colour. The dish should be the consistency of a dense broth
10. Turn off heat and serve with the bread, olive oil, sea salt, and lemons, in the centre of the table for each diner to garnish their portion to taste

Λευκά
Φασόλια

Warm White Cannellini Bean Salad

Λευκά Φασόλια

Cannellini beans or 'fasolia' are a legume. They are often confused with cannellini, which is a type of pasta. Eating cannellini has many health benefits, including lowering cholesterol. They have a mild nutty flavour. Cook them until they are soft, creamy, and fluffy. This is essentially a stew, although a 'warm salad' best describes the finished dish. It is usually consumed at room temperature. A very common and traditional Cypriot meal, the ingredients are very simple and economical. They are enhanced by the carrots, celery and then crowned with extra virgin olive oil, chopped fresh parsley, and lemon juice.

Preparing the Salad

- 500g Dry canellinni beans (soaked overnight)
- 6-8 Celery stalks. Thickly slice the celery and include the leaves as they add an additional sweetness. Discard any outer stalks with fibrous ribs
- 2-3 Large carrots. Peel, discard top and bottom stalks, and chop into thick slices

Dressing

- ½ Cup extra virgin olive oil
- 3 Lemons. Cut into halves

Garnish

- 20g Flat leaf parsley. Rinse, dry and chop coarsely
- 1 Small onion. Peel and cut into eight pieces

Cooking Method

1. Drain the soaking liquid from the beans and immerse in a saucepan of water. Bring to the boil and cook rapidly for 20 minutes. Keep an eye out for the volcano of scum to erupt. Drain the beans and rinse the pan clean. Wipe the sides with a clean damp cloth if necessary. Cover generously with hot water and continue to boil for a further 15 minutes

2. Drain the beans. Cover them generously with hot water and continue to boil on a medium heat for a further 35 minutes or until they begin to soften. Stir occasionally and remove any scum from the surface of the liquid. Do not allow to boil dry

3. When the beans are soft, add the celery and continue to cook on a medium heat for 10 minutes

4. Add the carrots and salt to taste. Cook until all the vegetables are completely tender and the beans are fluffy and creamy. The consistency should be similar to a dense broth

5. Turn off heat. Divide into portions, and place the dressings, garnishes, and bread in the centre of the table so that your diners may help themselves.

Serve with crusty bread to mop up all those delicious juices.

> **Top Tip.**
> Be generous with the oil and lemon - and perhaps - a pinch of sea salt - Cypriot style. If you find your beans are breaking up and beginning to lose their shape, add the salt and other vegetables sooner.

Footnote.
Although this dish is a salad, it can be eaten hot, cold, or room temperature.

Φασόλια Γιαχνί

Flavoursome Fasolia Yiachni

Φασόλια Γιαχνί

A dish by no other name, 'fasolia' is the Greek name for cannellini beans; 'yiachni' is to stew in olive oil, tomatoes, and onions. As the name suggests, it tastes mellow, yet fully balanced and very satisfying. This dish is traditional, authentic, and notoriously good. It is a supreme vegan fasting dish of Cypriots. Almost every family will prepare this – whether fasting or not. It is a triple gold-winning recipe. It tastes great, is inexpensive, simple to prepare, nutritious, and accommodating of many dietary requirements. It is almost beyond belief how a dish with so few ingredients and with very little effort can be as good as it is. This is the dish to wean your vegetable and legume-hating fussy eaters.

Soaking Time Overnight

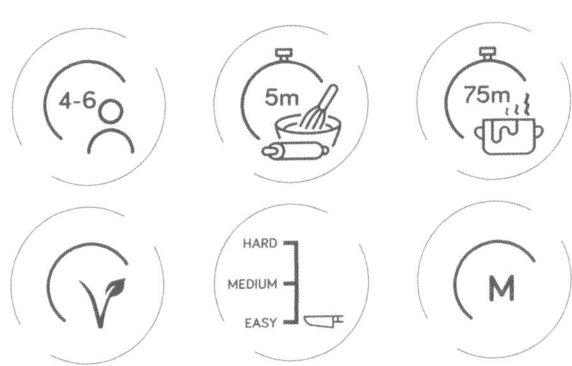

Preparing the Yiachni

- 500g Dry raw cannellini beans. Immerse in cold water. Soak overnight
- 6-8 Celery stalks with leaves if possible. Trim top and bottom of stalks, rinse, and cut into large pieces
- 2 Large carrots. Peel, discard top and bottom stalks, rinse, and cut into pieces of a similar thickness to the celery
- 1 Large onion. Peel and roughly chop
- 200-250ml Light olive oil
- 50ml Extra virgin olive oil
- 400g Tomato pasatta or tinned chopped tomatoes
- 3 Tbsp tomato purée
- Salt and freshly ground pepper to taste

> **Top Tip.**
> Add salt sooner into the cooking time if your beans are becoming too soft before dish is finished to prevent them breaking up.

Footnote.
Soaking overnight, changing the water twice, fast boiling, and cooking the beans really well all contribute to making them far more digestible. In fact, we do not attribute bloated tummies to well-cooked legumes.

Cooking Method

1. Drain the soaked cannellini beans, and then pour into a large saucepan and immerse in water. Bring to the boil and cook rapidly for 20 minutes. Keep an eye out for the volcano of scum to erupt. Drain the beans, rinse the pan clean, and wipe the sides with a clean damp cloth if necessary. Then, cover generously with hot water and continue to boil for a further 15 minutes

2. Drain the beans. Cover generously with hot water and continue to boil on a medium heat for a further 35 minutes or until they begin to soften. Stir occasionally with a wooden spoon and skim off any froth from the surface. Do not allow to boil dry

3. Pour the oil into a separate small saucepan on a medium heat. When the oil is heated through (not boiling hot) stir in the onions, season with salt, and turn down heat to low. Sauté the onions for 10-12 minutes until they are tender. Stir frequently and allow the onions to take on an evenly light golden colour. Take care not to burn them as they will become bitter. When the onions are cooked, grind freshly ground pepper into the pan and take off the heat

4. Stir the celery and carrots in to the beans. Season with salt to taste and continue to simmer on a medium heat for another 15-20 minutes or until the beans are creamy and the vegetables are very soft

5. Stir the tomato pasatta and tomato purée into the caramelised fried onions. Take a cupful of liquid from the beans and leave to one side. Stir the onions into the beans, pour the cupful of liquid into the pan, in which you fried the onions to deglaze it, and then pour this into the beans

6. Simmer gently on a low heat for a further 10-15 minutes, stirring every 3-4 minutes. When the colour deepens and becomes uniform and the vegetables and beans are completely soft, then the dish is ready. Taste, and adjust seasoning if necessary. Turn off heat and put the lid on. Let it rest for 10 minutes, as the beans will absorb a little more liquid and the flavours will blend. It will remain hot for at least 1 hour

Serve with crusty bread, black olives, and slithers of raw onion for very authentic accompaniments to this dish.

Ρεβίδια
Πιλάφι

Cheap as Chips Chickpea Stew

Ρεβίδια Γιαχνί

Chickpeas, characterised as a legume, are tradtionally well-used ingredients, as they are a wholesome alternative to protein and far more accessible. Meat was unaffordable for many of the hard-working Cypriot small holders. In fact, it was more usual that meat was reserved for special occasions and celebrations. The cooks were masters of developing techniques to prepare the most ordinary produce with the addition of a few humble ingredients. There were more often than not hand picked daily from their own farms. In this way, they transformed the bland into appetising dishes that would be enjoyed by the whole family. This chickpea stew epitomises all of the above requirements to a very high degree.

Preparing the Stew

- 500g Dry chickpeas
- 5 Tbsp light olive oil
- 1 Large onion. Peel and roughly chop
- 1 Large carrot. Discard top and bottom stalks, peel, rinse, and cut into thick slices
- 2 Celery sticks. Rinse, trim top and bottom of each stalk, discard any fibrous string, cut in half lengthwise, and then cut into thick slices
- 400g Tinned chopped tomatoes
- 1 Tbsp tomato purée
- 1 Vegetable stock cube suitable for vegans
- ½ Tsp dry cumin
- ½ Tsp ground cinnamon
- Salt and freshly ground pepper

Garnish

- Chopped flat leaf parsley

Cooking Method

1. Drain the cooking liquid from the chickpeas
2. Boil a kettle full of water
3. Pour chickpeas into a saucepan, cover generously with water, and bring to the boil on a high heat. Boil until a volcano of scum begins to erupt. Drain the water, rinse any residue from the saucepan, and wipe with a clean damp cloth if necessary, add the chickpeas back to the pan and cover generously with water
4. Repeat step 3, and continue to boil for 60 minutes on a medium heat and stir frequently. Do not let the chickpeas boil dry; they should be covered by twice their volume of water
5. Heat another saucepan on medium heat. Add the oil and the onions, and sauté until they are evenly golden brown. Do not overcook the onions, as they will become bitter
6. Stir in the cumin/cinnamon. Then, follow quickly with the tomatoes and continue to cook for 2-3 minutes. Turn off heat
7. When the chickpeas are soft and plump, add the celery and carrots and season with salt to taste. Take one cup of broth from the chickpea pan, Put to one side
8. Add the onions/tomatoes to the chickpeas. Pour the broth into the pan, in which you fried the onions, to deglaze, stir the stock cube in to dissolve it. Add this to the chickpeas, season with pepper to taste, and continue to simmer on a low heat for 10-15 minutes. Stir frequently
9. Cook until the redness of the tomatoes deepens and becomes uniform. The liquid should reduce by 1/3 and the chickpeas should be melt in your mouth. Check the seasoning and adjust if necessary. Allow the dish to rest for 10 minutes with a lid on, before serving

Footnote.
I have used tinned chickpeas on occasion. Reduce the cooking time at step 4, then follow recipe.

Serve with crusty bread, black olives, and slithers of raw onion or a feta salad.

Κουκιά με
Σέσκουλα

Swiss Chard & Broad Bean Salad

Κουκιά με Σέσκουλο

This is typically a peasant dish, which requires very simple and inexpensive ingredients. It is a warm salad which, pairs a winning combination of sweet and crunchy stems of chard - including their slightly bitter leaves with buttery broad beans. This is married with generous helpings of extra virgin olive oil and lemon juice, which elevate this delicate dish into something really unique. We Greeks always serve this salad alongside homemade artisan bread - always an essential ingredient in the larder. Failing this, I serve it with shop bought sourdough bread which is most similar to the bread made back home.

   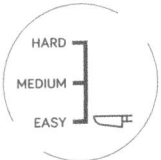  

Preparing the Salad

- 200g Frozen, fresh, or dry broad beans (see footnote)
- 200g Swiss or rainbow chard. Trim stalks, rinse well, discard any fibrous ribs of the stalk, and chop the chard into the desired sizes
- Salt and freshly ground pepper to taste

Dressing
- 80g Extra virgin olive oil
- 1 Large lemon

Cooking Method

1. Add the chard to a saucepan. Completely cover with cold water, bring to the boil, turn down heat to medium, and cook for 3-4 minutes
2. Add the frozen beans to the pan, salt to taste, and continue to simmer for 6-8 minutes. There should be enough water to cover the ingredients. This will also serve as your dressing
3. Take off the heat, allow to cool for 10 minutes, and divide into portions. Add a little cooking liquid, dress with oil, lemon juice, and seasoning to taste

Footnote.
Replace frozen beans with fresh, when they are in season from April until mid September. To prepare fresh beans, simply shed the beans from their pods and then cook as the recipe states. No self respecting Greek cook skins fresh fava/broad beans, but if you must, blanche beans for one minute in hot water. Then drain, immerse in cold water, drain again, and remove skins by pressing gently with your fingers against the sides of the beans. Then cook the beans as this recipe states.
If using dry broad beans, follow the instructions on the packaging, before you follow the recipe.

Top Tip.
To make chopping easier, roll the chard into a cigar shape, and then cut.

Φασολάκι
Γιαχνί

Green Bean & Potato Stew

Φασολάκι Γιαχνί

A huge variety of vegetables, legumes, pulses, and meat are prepared this way. It is a very traditional and popular recipe that remains a timeless classic. Years ago, I would sit with a tray full of fresh green beans on my lap for what seemed an endless amount of time, top, tailing, and removing the inedible fibrous 'string' that the old varieties of green beans used to have running down one side. Thanks to our growers, most modern varieties of beans do not have them. These days, however, I often use frozen beans as I like the convenience. In common with frozen peas, they are just as good as fresh. Green beans or 'fasolaki' are transformed from a vegetable side dish, which is often left on the plate, to a celebrated ingredient that you will look forward to eating. Joy of joys - this dish is a one-pot simple recipe that takes very little effort. Cook until the beans are soft and dark green in colour. No squeaky beans please.

   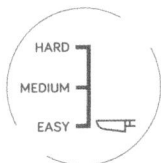  

Preparing the Stew

- 1kg Frozen fine whole green beans
- 3 Large potatoes. Peel and chop into quarters
- 2 Onions. Peel and roughly chopped
- 1 Large carrot. Peel and cut into thick slices
- 300g Tomato passata or tinned chopped tomatoes
- 80ml Light olive oil
- 1 Tbsp tomato purée
- 1 Vegetable/vegan stock cube, dissolved
- ½ Tsp ground cinammon
- Salt and pepper to taste
- Water

Cooking Method

1. Heat a large pan on a medium heat. Add the oil, continue to heat, then add the onions, season with salt, and sauté for 6-8 minutes or until they take on a little colour and are completely soft

2. Stir in the tomatoes, tomato purée, and ground cinnamon

3. Add the potatoes to the pan and stir well to coat them in the oil and tomatoes. Add the still-frozen green beans and the carrots to the pan on top of the potatoes

4. Dissolve the stock in the water and pour into the pan. The water should just come up past the potatoes. Adjust the amount of water if necessary. Bring to the boil

5. Season and continue to cook on a medium heat, with a lid on, until the potatoes and green beans are completely soft. The consistency should be similar to a stew. Do not boil dry

6. Gently shake the pan from side to side 3-4 times during cooking to prevent the potatoes from sticking to pan and to help mix the flavours

7. Check the seasoning. Turn off the heat and allow the dish to settle for 10 minutes before serving

Serve with crusty bread and olives.

Footnote.
The beans may not look as appetising as undercooked beans, but they will taste far better when well cooked, as they absorb more flavour from the cooking liquid.

Top Tip.
You can swap the frozen beans with fresh topped and tailed green beans if you prefer. However, this can be more expensive, as you require 1kg of them. Alternatively, can use frozen garden peas instead or a combination of both.

Σαλάτες

Salads

Ταμπούλι

Greek style Tabbouleh

Ταμπούλι

Several 'tabbouleh' recipes were introduced to the Cypriots by the Lebanese, many of whom migrated to Cyprus bringing their delicious cuisine with them. These delicious recipes were easily adopted and made our own. This is my preferred recipe - not least as it is so simple to prepare. Cypriot households call the cous cous grain 'semolina'. They are both a precooked durum wheat and sometimes use fine ground bulgar wheat instead. This recipe requires absolutely no cooking apart from boiling a kettle! It is packed full of Mediterranean flavours and will get your taste buds tingling.

   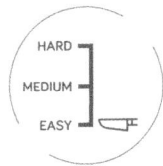  

Preparing the Cous Cous

Salad
- 220g Cous cous
- 20–30g Flat leaf parsley. Rinse, dry and finely chop
- 20–30g Fresh mint leaves, rinsed, dried and finely chopped, or 1 heaped tsp dried mint
- 2 Medium tomatoes. Discard cores and cut into dice (save any tomato juices)
- 1 Small red onion. Peel and finely chop
- ½ Cucumber. Peel and cut in half lengthwise. Scoop out soft middle with a tsp and finely dice
- 1 Large lemon, juiced
- 1 Tbsp extra virgin olive oil

Stock
- 1 Vegan or vegetable stock cube
- 1 Tsp light olive oil
- 300ml Hot water
- Pinch of salt
- Freshly ground pepper to taste

Cooking Method

1. Boil the kettle and measure out the hot water required to make up the stock
2. Add the stock cube, 1 tsp of light olive oil, and salt and pepper to the water, and stir to dissolve stock cube. Add the saved tomato juices as well
3. Pour the cous cous into a large bowl and pour over the stock. Stir well to completely immerse the cous cous in the stock. Cover with cling film and leave to one side for 10 minutes
4. When all the stock has been absorbed, lightly fork through the cous cous
5. Add the remaining ingredients, 1 tbsp of extra virgin olive oil, and ¾ of the lemon juice. Gently mix until all ingredients are evenly distributed. Taste and add the remaining lemon juice and more salt and pepper if required
6. Refrigerate for 1 hour before serving

Serve with any of the following: grilled halloumi, seasoned and grilled large flat mushrooms, hummus, warmed pitta bread, and any dip of your choice.

Trouble shooting.
Oven timings and temperature are based on the use of fan ovens. Adjust timings accordingly if you are using a conventional oven.

Footnote.
Cool and refrigerate as soon as possible. Consume leftovers within 2 days.

Top Tip.
You can use spring onion instead of red onion if you prefer.

Πατατοσαλάτα

Fresh Parsley & Potato Salad

Πατατοσαλάτα

Cypriot potatoes are remarkably good. In fact, they are so exceptional that they are widely used commercially. Here, in the UK, you will probably have eaten them without knowing, as they are the biggest export from Cyprus to the UK. They are used by many UK manufacturers for crisps and chips. So, it should come as no surprise, that when you eat a dish with Cypriot potatoes, the taste is divine. There are many varieties of Cypriot potatoes - Spunta, Marfona, Diamant are just a few that you may have eaten. The Charlotte variety is great for this recipe, as there is no need to peel them. Alternatively, any small waxy salad potato, that is suitable for boiling with the skins on, will do.

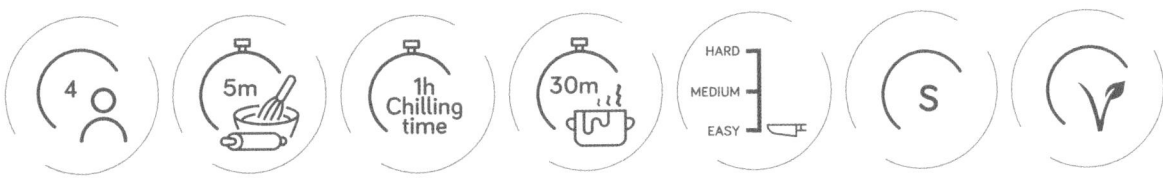

Preparing the Salad

Salad
- 500g Waxy potatoes, such as Charlotte or Anya
- 20-30g Fresh flat leaf parsley. Rinsed, dry, and finely chop

Dressing
- 2 Large cloves of garlic. Peel and mince
- 4-5 Tbsp extra virgin olive oil
- 1-2 Large lemons, juiced. Discard pips
- Salt and freshly ground pepper to taste

Cooking Method

1. Scrub potatoes in a bowl of cold water, then rinse well
2. Leave the smaller potatoes whole, and cut the larger ones in half crosswise, so that they are roughly the same size
3. Put potatoes in a saucepan of hot salted water on a medium to high heat and bring to the boil. Then, turn down to a medium heat and continue to cook for about 20 minutes or until they are soft yet still holding their shape. Test by inserting a fork
4. Drain potatoes and allow them to cool for 10 minutes before dressing
5. Place the potatoes in a bowl and add ¾ of the lemon juice, the parsley, minced garlic, olive oil, and a little freshly ground pepper and salt to taste
6. Mix carefully until all the potatoes are well coated in the dressing. Taste and add the remaining lemon juice if you wish

Serve with dips, olives, warm pitta bread, beetroot salad, boiled eggs, or grilled halloumi.

Top Tip.
If you are making this dish in advance, refrigerate the cooked potatoes and dress just before serving. The garlic turns green, when it comes into contact with warm potatoes and oil, and then refrigerated.

Φέτα
Σαλάτα

Fanciful Feta Salad

Φέτα Σαλάτα

Greeks have made feta cheese for thousands of years. It is a crumbly brined cheese, which is made in large blocks and then cut into 'fettes'. 'Fettes' means slices, which is why it is called feta cheese. I am blessed to have watched my 'yiayia'-Grandmother make cheese by hand in her utility room in Cyprus. The walls where lined wall to wall with urns ready to hold the next batch of milk from the family's tribe of goats. Feta was stored alongside the urns in wooden barrels filled with brine. My grandmother would give the lucky onlookers a small dish of the fresh curds-'anari', which is a by-product of the whey or liquid from the making of fresh cheese. Whilst still warm, this would be sprinkled with a little sugar and ground cinnamon - to be eaten whilst she continued to hand form the halloumi and feta cheeses. It was such a long and labour-intensive procedure. However, it necessary, as these where the days where shops where hard to come by. Futhermore, the expense of feeding large families forced the villagers to utilise every edible ingredient, which their farms and animals yielded. This included making the indispensable staple of bread by hand. Today, you can easily source feta cheese. Check the label for its origins, as Greek feta is far superior in taste. There are also vegan alternatives for feta which you can use for this recipe.

  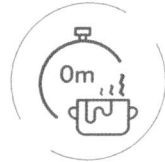 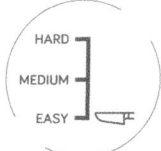  

Preparing the Salad

- 200g Greek feta cheese or vegan substitute
- 2-3 Large ripe tomatoes, stored at room temperature. Discard cores, halve and slice
- ½ Whole cucumber. Halve lengthwise. Discard soft centre with a small spoon and chop into half moons
- 1 Large red onion. Peel and finely slice
- 8-10 Black olives. Unpitted kalamata olives are the authentic choice
- ½ Tsp dried oregano
- 2 Tbsp extra virgin olive oil
- ½ Fresh lemon, juiced, or 1 tbsp of red/white vinegar to taste
- Freshly ground pepper to taste
- 3-4 Fresh mint leaves. Rinse, pat dry, finely slice. Alternatively, use ½ tsp dried mint

Cooking Method

1. Place the onion, tomatoes, and cucumber in a bowl and dress with lemon juice and pepper to taste. Add ¾ of the olive oil and mix gently. Pour onto a flat serving dish or bowl and even out the ingredients

2. Place the block of feta cheese on top and drizzle with the remaining oil. Sprinkle the feta with the oregano and mint

3. Place the olives around the feta cheese and serve straight away

Serve with warmed pitta breads, koubebia/dolmades and dips.

> **Top Tip.**
> If you want to make this a little in advance, prepare ingredients, and assemble and dress the salad when you are ready to serve. I do not add salt to my feta salad, as the olives and feta cheese are very salty. However, can add it if you like - sea salt would be best.

Εποχιακή Σαλάτα

Seasonal Garden Salad

Εποχιακή Σαλάτα

All my children love salad, and I attribute this to the village salads which we ate whilst on holiday. I then replicated them as best I could, once home. The key to a good salad is quite simply in the dressing. A salad without dressing is the same as any other dish that you have not seasoned - bland, unappetising and boring. Treat your salad with a little attention and it will soon become your 'go to' side dish with meals. At home, the salad is served as the main dish next to rice, grilled large flat mushrooms, grilled vegetables, meat, or fish. Simply incorporate as many fresh seasonal salad items as you please. As you can see from the long ingredients list, I treat a salad with as much consideration as any main dish. Do not be deterred, as it is well worth the effort - and there is no cooking involved.

Cooking Method

I rinse all my salad ingredients to minimise any risk of contamination - irrespective of whether the product is 'washed and ready to use'

1. Discard outer leaves of lettuce, rinse, and place upright in colander to drain
2. Rinse fresh coriander and place in colander to drain
3. Rinse the rocket leaves and place on a tea towel to dry
4. Rinse cucumber, cut in half lengthwise, and use a small spoon to remove and discard the soft centre
5. Rinse tomatoes, pat dry using a kitchen towel, cut in half, and discard the core
6. Discard thick fibrous core of white cabbage, any thick ribs, and the outer leaves. Leave to one side
7. Remove the outer fibrous celery stalks and save for homemade stock. Alternatively, peel them with a vegetable peeler to remove fibrous ribs, rinse and pat dry, cut in quarter lengthwise, and trim off top and bottom of stalks. Do not discard leaves. Add these to the salad
8. Rinse pepper and pat dry. Cut in half, discard core, stem, seeds, and white pith
9. Slice the cabbage as thinly as possible in to a large mixing bowl
10. Cut the celery stalks into thin slices - leaves and all, and add to the bowl. The tender heart/stem of the celery is sweet and crunchy. It is the cook's treat. Nibble on it as you cut the rest of the salad
11. Slice the pepper in to thin slices and add to the bowl
12. Halve the onions, slice finely, and then add to the bowl
13. Cut the cucumber into half lengthwise and chop into small slices
14. Cut the halved tomatoes into ¼ and add to the bowl
15. Ensure the lettuce, fresh coriander, and rocket leaves are completely dry. Give them a pat with a paper kitchen towel if necessary. Add the rocket leaves to the bowl. Roughly chop the coriander, and add to the bowl. Separate the lettuce leaves, slice finely, and add to the bowl. Discard the heart/stem, as it is bitter
16. Add the drained olives to the bowl
17. Generously dress with extra virgin olive, dried mint, or oregano. Then, add salt and lemon juice to taste. Mix well to evenly coat all the salad with the dressing. You can, at this point, transfer your salad to a serving bowl or individual dishes if you like
18. Top the salad with the caper berries and caper stems

Serve with vermicelli rice or Bulgur Wheat Pilaf, dips, and warmed pitta breads. In fact, we serve this salad with almost everything, or top with feta cheese or grilled halloumi.

Preparing the Salad

Salad

- ½ Small white cabbage
- ½ Whole cucumber
- 2 Ripe tomatoes, kept at room temperature
- 1 Romaine lettuce
- 40g Rocket leaves
- ¼ Whole celery
- 15g Fresh coriander or flat leaf parsley
- 1 Small red onion, peeled
- 1 Small pepper (red, yellow, or orange)
- 1 Fresh lemon, juiced to taste
- 2 Tsp pickled caper berries
- 3-4 Stems of pickled caper stems
- 8-10 Black olives. Kalamata with pips are traditional

Dressing

- 1 Large lemon, juiced to taste. Alternatively, use 2-3 tbsp red wine vinegar
- 4-6 Tbsps extra virgin olive oil
- Salt to taste
- ½ Tsp dried oregano or mint

Footnote.
The wide variety of ingredients make this salad great. You can, however, adapt it to the ingredients you have in your fridge. One ingredient, which is essential for a good salad, is extra virgin olive oil. You can also make this a little in advance by preparing all the ingredients, placing the lighter leaves on top. Dress and toss in a large mixing bowl, and transfer to a serving bowl, just before you serve.

Παντζαροσαλάτα

Beautiful Beetroot salad

Παντζαροσαλάτα

Cypriots have grown beetroot on their allotments for years. It is harvested when in season, and pickled or brined to be preserved all year round. The simplest dishes are the best - and this is one of them! I simplify it further by using pre-cooked vacuum-packed beetroot and pre-packaged pomegranate seeds found in the fruit isle, feel free to boil your own beetroot if you prefer. Rinse and scrub the raw beetroot in a bowl of cold water. Then rinse with clean water, and boil in hot water for 30–40 minutes or until you can pierce the centre with a knife. I call this 'beautiful beetroot salad', as it is looks as beautiful as it tastes.

   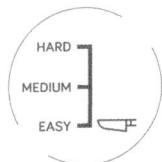  

Preparing the Salad

Salad
- 8 Beetroots -precooked and vacuum-packed
- 250g Pre-packed pomegranate seeds or a fresh pomegranate. Discard peel and pith
- 1 Large clove of garlic. Peeled and mince

Dressing
- 3-4 Tbsp extra virgin olive oil
- ½ Lemon, juiced. Discard pips
- 1 Tbsp red wine vinegar
- 1 Tsp dried mint (optional)
- Salt to taste

Cooking Method

1. Chop the beetroot into large similar-sized dice. Place in a bowl
2. Add the pomegranate seeds to the bowl
3. Add the dressing ingredients. Gently coat and adjust the seasonings to taste
4. Chill for 30 minutes before serving

Serve with dips, 'Not Kleftico' or potato salad. Greek yoghurt, warm pitta bread, and olives

Footnote.
If you are using pickled beetroot, reduce the amount of lemon juice and vinegar in the dressing, to taste.

Top Tip.
Wear gloves suitable for food use, before handling beetroot.

Dips

Dips have become a mainstay of the Greek diet. They customarily accompany our meals and help to make up the various little dishes known as 'meze', which suit the way we like to eat. Every day, we look out for an unusual or special ingredient. This could be freshly-foraged asparagus, mushrooms, or wild greens, as well as cucumber, or tomatoes fresh from the allotment. Other options may be warmed pitta or loaf of bread, olives and any amount of crudités and pickles. Irrespective of the simplicity of the ingredients, you can be assured that meal times are always something we Cypriots look forward to.

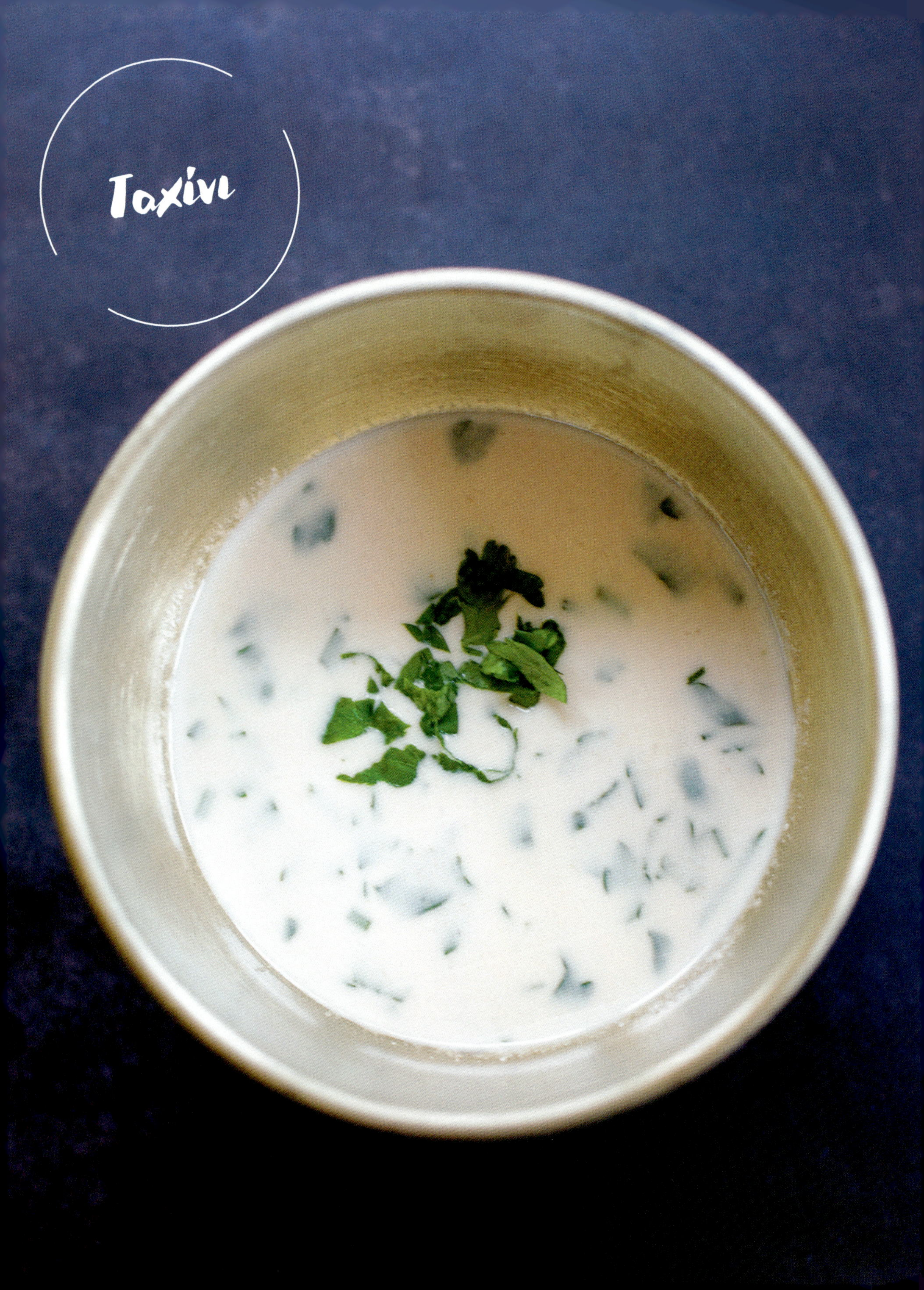
Ταχίνι

Tahini Dip

Taxívi

'Tahini' is probably one of the lesser recognised dips. Although you are likely to know that it is an ingredient in hummus, it is made from ground sesame seeds. In Cyprus, it is commonly served with fish in those lovely beach-side fish restaurants that the locals and tourists frequent. 'Tahini' has an earthy, nutty flavour, which is really livened up with lemon and garlic. It is a delicious dip which is great with crudités, any type of bread, and as a salad dressing. It is also used in baking and for halva.

  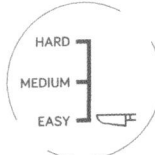  

Preparing the Dip

- 150g Greek tahini paste, shop-bought
- 70ml Warm water
- 2-3 Large garlic cloves. Peel and mince
- 1-2 Large lemons, juiced
- 35ml Extra virgin olive oil
- 15g Flat leaf parsley. Rinse, pat dry, and finely chop
- Salt to taste

Cooking Method

1. Add the tahini paste to a mixing bowl. Add the water - a little at a time, and, using a hand-balloon whisk or an electric-hand whisk, whisk for 2-3 minutes until it is well combined and lightens in colour and texture

2. Add ½ of the lemon juice and whisk for a another minute. Taste and add more lemon if required

3. Add the olive oil, garlic, and salt to taste and whisk for another minute or two

4. Taste, add more salt and olive oil if required. If the dip is too thick for your liking, add a little more cool water or lemon juice, and whisk again

5. Stir in the parsley and chill before serving

Serve as part of a meze dish. Alternatively, drizzle over salads and vegetables, or use as a garnish on any of the legume or pulse dishes.

> **Top Tip.**
> Tahini thickens a little as it cools. Do not add lemon before water, as this thickens the tahini paste and makes it hard to combine.

Τζατζίκι

Ταλατούρι

Tsatsiki Dip or Talatouri Dip

Τζατζίκι η Ταλατούρι

'Tsatsiki' is a dip with a base of fresh cooling plain Greek yoghurt, which is enhanced with garlic, white wine vinegar, and olive oil. Persia, the Middle East, and India, amongst others, have a version of this much-loved dip. In fact, Cyprus has two variations the other lesser-known 'relative' called 'talatouri'. This is my family's favourite as it has dried or fresh mint in the recipe. I will give you the recipe for both, and you can decide for yourselves which you like best.

   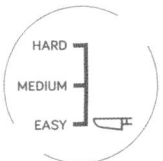  

Preparing the Dip

Tsatsiki dip

- 500g Plain Greek yoghurt
- 2 Garlic cloves. Peel and mince
- ½ Whole cucumber
- 3 Tsp white wine vinegar
- ¼ Cup extra virgin olive oil
- Pinch of salt

Talatouri dip

- 500g Plain Greek yogurt
- 2 Garlic cloves. Peel and mince
- ½ Cucumber
- 1 Lemon, juiced. No pips
- ¼ Cup extra virgin olive oil
- 2-3 Tsp dried mint or 80g fresh mint, rinsed, dried and finely chopped
- Pinch of salt

Cooking Method

Method for tsatsiki

1. Rinse the cucumber. Cut in half lengthwise, deseed the soft centre with a small spoon, and discard
2. Grate the cucumber on the large side of box grater, place in a sieve or clean kitchen towel, and squeeze out as much of the moisture as possible
3. Put in a mixing bowl and stir in the yoghurt, garlic, oil, and a pinch of salt
4. Stir in the white wine vinegar
5. Mix well. Taste and refrigerate until well chilled before serving

Method for talatouri dip

Follow Steps 1-3 of tsatsiki recipe then:

1. Stir in the lemon juice and mint
2. Taste, adjust if necessary, and then refrigerate

Serve with warmed pitta breads.

> **Top Tip.**
> You can use fresh, dried mint, or even mint sauce, although this method will give your yoghurt a green tinge. These can be made in advance and stored in an airtight container for up two days.

Χούμους

Humous

Χούμους

Humous is a hugely-popular and widely-available dip - made from chickpeas and tahini paste. The Cypriots traded many commodities, ingredients, and recipes with neighbouring countries - not least of which this recipe for humous. It was adopted from the Egyptians as far back as the 13th Century. Greeks believed that the Egyptians introduced it to the Middle Eastern/Mediterranean merchants, with whom they conducted business. Regardless of its origins, it tastes splendid and is a versatile dip for every meal, or as part of a healthy snack.

   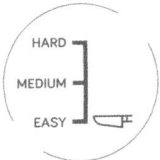  

Preparing the Dip

- 400g Tin cooked chickpeas
- Large garlic cloves
- 1 Tbsp fresh lemon juice
- 1-2 Tbsp tahini paste (shop bought)
- 2-3 Tbsp extra virgin olive oil
- Salt to taste

Garnish (optional)

- Lightly toasted pine nuts
- Dried paprika
- Dried oregano
- Cayenne pepper (if you like hot spice)

Cooking Method

1. Drain and rinse the chickpeas under cold running water. Place in a sieve or colander to dry
2. Blend all the ingredients together - either with a hand blender or a food processor. Add the lemon juice to taste (do not add the garnish)
3. Taste. Adjust accordingly
4. If the humous is too thick for your taste, add a little water or more lemon juice
5. Refrigerate

Footnote.
You can use dry chickpeas. Cook as per instructions on the packaging and then follow this recipe.

N.B
Retain the juice from the tinned chickpeas, and make the vegan chocolate mousse recipe featured on page 8

Top Tip.
Can be made in advance and stored in an airtight container for up to 3 days in the fridge.

Σκορδαλιά

Skordalia Garlic Potato Dip

Σκορδαλιά

The word 'skordalia' is derived from the word 'skordo', which means garlic in Greek. This is the Greek adaptation of mashed potato. Although technically a dip, it is often used as a side dish to fried cod, called 'pakaliaros'. This garlic and lemon dip complements and enhances fried fish or tempura vegetables beautifully. Serve warm from the pan or chilled according to your preference.

Preparing the Dip

- 500g Floury potatoes, such as Cyprus, Maris Piper, King Edwards
- 2-3 Large garlic cloves, peeled and minced
- 140ml Extra virgin olive oil
- 1 Spring onion. Remove outer leaves. Trim stalks, discard green fibrous stems, rinse, and finely chop
- 30g Flat leaf parsley. Rinse, pat dry, and finely chop
- 1 Small lemon, juiced or 2-3 Tbsp white wine vinegar
- Salt and freshly ground pepper

Cooking Method

1. Peel and rinse potatoes. Chop into large dice roughly the same size
2. Add the potatoes to a saucepan of hot salted water. Boil until soft but not breaking up. Drain into a colander, and then stand over the warm pan to dry. These steps make the mash less starchy, and light and fluffy
3. Add the garlic, salt, and pepper to a mortar and pestle. Grind until you have a smooth paste. Stir in the lemon juice
4. Pour the drained potatoes into a bowl or the drained saucepan, and mash until as smooth as possible
5. Add the oil, a little at a time, whilst mixing vigorously. Continue to add the oil until you achieve the consistency and texture that you require. Do not be deterred by the colour, as the green hue is customary for a skordalia dip
6. Taste and then adjust seasoning accordingly
7. Stir in the spring onions and the parsley. Serve warm or refrigerate for later

Footnote.
You can add more oil to this recipe to achieve a more fluid consistency.

Top Tip.
If your mash splits/separates whilst you are adding the oil, add an ice cube or very cold water, a drop at a time and continue to stir.

Μελιτζανοσαλάτα

Aubergine Dip   Μελιτζανοσαλάτα

As aubergines cook, they become soft and moist, and taste incredible. This is why they are ideal as the main ingredient in this dish.

  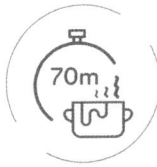 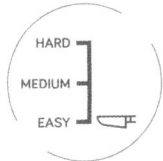  

Preparing the Dip

- 4 Large aubergines. Rinse and pat dry
- 2 Garlic cloves
- 30g Flat leaf parsley. Rinse, dry and chop very finely
- ½ Red onion. Peel and chop very finely
- 125ml Extra virgin olive oil
- 4 Tbsp fresh lemon juice
- Salt and freshly ground pepper to taste

Cooking Method

1. Preheat a fan oven to 200 degrees C
2. Cut each of the whole aubergines in half lengthwise. Make a few slits in the flesh of each of them, and then add a slice of the garlic in each slit. Place them skin side down on a baking tray, along with a splash of water, then place in the oven and bake for about 1 hour or until they are soft
3. Remove the cooked garlic stuffed aubergines from the oven. When they are cool enough to handle, scoop out the pulp into a mixing bowl, and mash with a fork or potato masher, or use a hand blender, to achieve the texture you would like as a dip
4. Add the rest of the ingredients to taste. Mix vigorously, taste, and adjust seasonings accordingly
5. Refrigerate for 1 hour or so before serving

Επιδόρπια

Desserts

Μαχαλεπί

Mahalepi Dessert

Μαχαλεπί

This is the epitome of a Cypriot dessert - a smooth, refreshingly light, and cooling set custard. It is unbelievably good, as it is made without the use of milk or eggs. When set the custard is garnished with rose water, rose cordial, ice cold water, and sugar to taste, it is absolutely scrumptious. You will find 'mahalepi' in all the village cafes - 'Καφενεία' during the wonderful long summer months. For the Greeks, this is a staple dessert when it is hot. For the locals, this dessert is as commonplace as having an ice cream. The cafes have this in the fridge, ready to serve to the regulars, whilst they play a game of backgammon called 'tavli'. Outlets, which specialise in this popular dessert, serve it to the locals, after they have had a long stroll or on a night out – 'peripato'.

Preparing the Mahalepi

Custard

- 50g Cornflour
- 1 Pint water
- 1 Tbsp rose water

Syrup

- 4 Tbsp rose water
- 150-200ml Rose cordial
- Jug of ice-cold water
- Sugar to taste

Cooking Method

1. Put ¼ of the water allocated to the custard in a saucepan. Add the cornflour and use a hand balloon whisk to mix it into a smooth paste

2. Whisk in all but ¼ of the remaining water. Turn on the heat to medium, and, whilst stirring, heat until it becomes a smooth custard

3. Turn down heat to very low. Gently simmer, whilst stirring for 12-15 minutes, until the custard is bubbling and translucent

4. Add the rose water and the remaining water, and then stir for 1-2 minutes longer. Turn off heat

5. Take four serving bowls and rinse with cold water. Do not dry but continue to divide the custard equally between the dishes using a spatula to scrape the sides of the pan clean

6. Leave the dishes to one side to cool for 20-30 minutes

7. Place the dishes in the fridge to chill for 4 hours or so

8. When you are ready to serve, place all the syrup ingredients in jugs. Allow each guest bowls, and to garnish their dish to taste with sugar, rose water, rose cordial, and ice-cold water. It is customary to cut the 'mahalepi' with your spoon and stir, so as to mix all the ingredients. This also dissolves the sugar prior to eating

> **Top Tip.**
> Double up this recipe. It will keep for up to 4 days in the fridge. It must be stored completely immersed in water. I make a large dish of this 1-½ cm thick, then refrigerate. When set, I gently pull the custard from the sides of the dish with clean fingers, and then coat the surface with cold water. Simply take out of the fridge, portion as you please, and garnish to taste.

Λιβανέζικη
Κρέμα

Levantine Cream

Λιβανέζικη Κρέμα

This delightfully-aromatic and simple dessert is, as the name implies, a rapturously-good recipe. It is actually a set custard, which was initially introduced to Cyprus by the Lebanese, whom we have embraced. It is easily made, with a great deal of fondness, to share when visiting friends and family, as it is customary to take something sweet for dessert when we do. It is a smooth and delicately-perfumed chilled set custard, bejewelled with crushed pistachio nuts.

   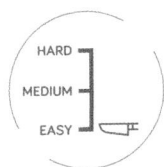  

Preparing the Levantine

Vegetarian Recipe

- 640ml Full-fat milk
- 500ml Fresh single cream
- 100g Sugar
- 6 Tbsp rose water
- 100g Cornflour
- 6 Pieces chios mastic resin
  (grind in a pestle and mortar with a little sugar)
- 60-80g Unsalted, shelled, and crushed pistachio nuts

Vegan Levantine Cream Recipe

Simply follow the vegetarian recipe, replacing the dairy milk with coconut, almond or oat milk, and replacing the dairy cream with vegan cream substitutes of your preference.

Cooking Method

1. Pour a little of the milk into a saucepan and add all the cornflour. Use a hand whisk to mix into a smooth paste
2. Add the remaining milk, cream, mastic resin, sugar, and rose water, and place on a low-medium heat. Continue to stir, using the whisk, and bring to the boil. Then turn down heat to low. Keep stirring and do not let the custard catch.
3. Simmer gently, stirring all the time, until you have a smooth, glossy, bubbling custard. Stir in 50g of cold water. Stir and turn off the heat
4. Being careful, as this is molten hot, divide into individual dishes, or to a 2-pint serving dish. Use a spatula to scrape out all the custard. Ensure you moisten your dish with cold water before you pour the custard
5. Cover with cling film, and then refrigerate for 6-8 hours
6. When firm set, sprinkle the Levantine custard with pistachios. Then, continue to chill until set firm

Μπακλαβάς

Mythical Baclava   Μπακλαβάς

Baclava was once the preserve enjoyed only by the rich, who where able to employ staff to prepare it. It was a hugely-laborious chore to make the paper thin pastry, and sugar was very expensive. It is a time-honoured Greek sweet/dessert, of which many Middle East and Mediterranean countries have their own beloved version. Nevertheless, baclava essentially consists of nuts, sweet syrup, and flaky filo pastry. Many use pistachio nuts, but the Cypriot way is to use a mixture of walnuts and almonds. Walnuts are grown in Cyprus in limited amounts, which makes them a really prized ingredient. The freshly-harvested, most tender, walnuts are used to make one of the most popular spoon sweets called 'karithaki yleeko'.

   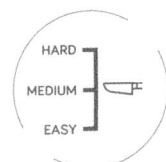 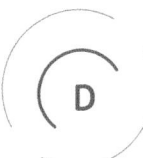 

Preparing the Baclava

You will need a shallow ovenproof dish 8" x 11"

Pastry and Filling

- 270g or 14 Sheets of shop-bought chilled filo pastry
- 400g Coarsely-ground, roughly-chopped, unsalted nuts, made up of 300g walnuts and 100g blanched almonds
- 1 Tbsp ground cinnamon
- 100g Sugar
- 1 Tbsp rose water
- 150g Melted butter, margarine or a vegan substitute

Syrup

- 400g Sugar
- 500ml Water
- 100g Honey or golden syrup
- 1 Small piece of cassia/cinnamon bark (Do not confuse with a cinnamon quill)
- 5-6 Whole spice cloves
- 2-3 Pieces of orange rind

Footnote.
Chopping the nuts very finely will make the finished baclava more delicate and refined.

Cooking Method

1. Make the syrup by putting all the ingredients for it into a small saucepan. Stir until the sugar dissolves. Turn on the heat and bring to the boil. Then, turn down heat and simmer for 12-14 minutes. Do not stir. Take off heat and allow to cool

2. Preheat fan oven to 180 degrees C

3. Add the chopped nuts, sugar, rose water, and cinnamon to a bowl, and stir to mix

4. Melt the butter and leave to one side

5. Take your chilled filo pastry out of the packaging and cover with a clean damp cloth to prevent it drying out

6. Use a pastry brush to butter your dish. Then, cover the base with 1/3 (roughly 4-5 sheets) of the filo. Brush each piece of the filo with some of the melted butter

7. Spread 1/3 of the nut mixture onto the filo in the dish, extending it out to the sides and patting it down very gently

8. Cover nut mixture with 1 sheet of filo, tucking in any excess, so that it does not have any overhanging pastry. Do not brush the filo with butter

9. Repeat step 8 twice more, until you have used all the nut mixture. Take care to evenly spread the remaining nut mixture into the dish, extending it out to the sides. Again, do not brush the filo pastry with butter

10. Add the remaining filo to the dish, one layer at a time, brushing each with butter. Repeat until you have used all the filo and the melted butter. Ensure that you butter the last surface layer of pastry

11. Take a sharp knife and score the surface of the pastry to mark out any shape you like, such as diamonds, triangles, or squares. These can be any size you like. Do not cut down to the nuts. Bear in mind that these scores are a template for your portions when the dish comes out of the oven

12. Pour any remaining butter down the sides of the dish. Sprinkle a few drops of cold water, with clean hands, onto the surface of the pastry, and place in the oven. Bake for roughly 60 minutes. Keep an eye on the dish to ensure the baclava does not brown too quickly

13. After 60 minutes, turn down oven to 150 degrees C. Then, continue to cook for a further 15 minutes. This will bake the baclava without burning, and give the dish a flaky finish

14. Take the dish out of the oven. Spoon ½ of the cold syrup over the baclava. Then, allow to rest for 2-3 minutes, before spooning over the remaining syrup, discarding the spice, bark, and rind

15. Cut through the baclava with a sharp knife, using the lines you made earlier as your guide. Let the baclava cool

16. When you are ready to serve, take out a corner portion of the baclava. If you feel there is too much syrup, slightly tilt the dish towards this space, and spoon out and discard the pool of syrup. Serve at room temperature or chilled from the fridge

Refrigerate leftovers. They will keep for up to three days in an airtight container.

Top Tip.
Check the dish after 40 minutes. If it is browning too quickly, turn down oven by 10-15 degrees.

Footnote.
The general rule for syrupy cakes and desserts is to add cold syrup to hot desserts, or vice versa.

Βραχάκια

Crispy Choc Pebbles

Βραχάκια

The underlying concept of this book was to jot down recipes and helpful tips that my children would use everyday to cook with their children or friends. It seemed only right, therefore, that I include this simple recipe for crispy chocolate pebbles, which we have all made together at some point over the years. Make them with your children and help them develop the skills they need to cook healthy, quick, and delicious meals.

    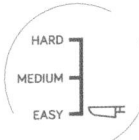  

Preparing the Pebbles

- 250g Chocolate of your choice
- 100g Crisped rice
- 40g Margarine or vegan alternative
- 50g Golden syrup
- 10-12 Cupcake cases

Cooking Method

1. Break chocolate into small pieces. Then, put them in a bowl over a pan of hot water, on a very low heat, and stir

2. When chocolate is melted, add the margarine and the golden syrup, and stir to combine

3. Turn off the heat and stir in the crisped rice

4. Divide mixture into cupcake cases and put them in the fridge. Chill for 1 hr

Top Tip.
Swap crisped rice with cornflakes, or add mini marshmallows, as a variation. For a more grown-up treat replace the cereal with nuts. Whole almonds, hazlenuts or Brazil's cut in quarters work well.

Ριζόγαλο
με Γάλα
Καρύδας

Coconut Milk Rice pudding

Ριζόγαλο με Γάλα Καρύδας

Rice pudding has become an international dish. Its travels have taken it to almost every corner of the world in some form or other. We Cypriots add orange rind, and scent it with rose water. Then, it is sprinkled with ground cinnamon and mostly consumed chilled. Coconut milk replaces dairy milk in this recipe. It is as though it was always meant to be the essential ingredient, and marries with the rice and cinnamon beautifully. Some recipes call for baking rice puddings in the oven, so that it forms a skin on top. This version is cooked on the hob so that it is soft, creamy, and fragrant.

   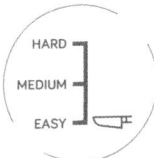 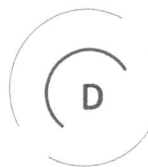 

Preparing the Pudding

- 600ml Fresh coconut milk
- 220ml Tinned coconut milk
- 1 Tbsp vanilla extract
- 1-2 Tbsp rose water (anthonero)
- 110g Pudding rice or arborio paella/risotto rice. Rinse, drain, and pick out any foreign matter
- 1 Stick of cinnamon/cassia bark
- 80-100g Sugar
- 2-3 Tsp ground cinnamon
- 2-3 Pieces orange rind, or zest the whole orange
- 250ml Water

Cooking Method

1. Place a saucepan over a medium heat. Add the rice and water. Stir with a wooden spoon until the rice begins to absorb the water

2. Turn down heat to low. Stir in the the fresh coconut milk, sugar, orange rind and cinnamon stick. Continue to stir until the rice begins to soften

3. Add the tinned coconut milk, rose water, and the vanilla extract. Taste, and add more sugar if you prefer. Continue to stir. If the rice is al dente at this point you should stir in a further 30-50ml of coconut milk (whichever you have left over). Simmer, whilst stirring, until the rice is completely soft and has absorbed most of the liquid. You are looking for a dropping consistency, for a soft, unxious-tasting pudding

4. Divide into serving bowls. Let them cool for 5-10 minutes, and sprinkle with as much ground cinnamon as you like. Then, chill before serving

Footnote.
Some believe that you should not rinse pudding rice, as it removes the starch, which makes it sticky. Cooking the rice until it is soft and creamy eliminates that problem.

Top Tip.
Of course, you can serve this warm if you prefer. Spoon warm rice pudding into dishes and serve with honey, golden syrup, jam, or any ripe berries. You can also swap the rose water with sweet orange blossom water.

Enticing Doughnuts

Ξεροτηγανα

There is a traditional vegan recipe for Greek-style sweet doughnuts, which are made in the run up to Christmas, when many of us are typically fasting. That said, I have modified the original recipe, which, in my view, makes these far simpler to prepare. Furthermore, the results are superior - both visually and taste wise. On the Greek island of Amorgos, they hold a festival in celebration of this vegan-friendly, fried, sweet pastry. Folklore has it that, in Cyprus, we burn incense and pray for the souls of 'Kalikantsari', which are ungodly, malevolent goblins. We make these doughnuts on the Epiphany, which falls on 6th January. We leave them on the doorstep as a bribe to entice the goblins - 'kalikantsari' out of our homes. The 'kalikantsari' are believed to live in the underworld, sawing away at 'The Tree of Life'. Accordingly, they come up above ground, during the run up to Christmas, to play tricks, uproot the Christmas tree, and cause all sorts of mischief. Traditional sausages called 'loucanika', along with small pieces of this pastry, are scattered, whilst singing a rhyming song. This song contains a verse that goes "Titchy titchy sausages and itsy bitsy dough for you nasty goblins to eat and go", which roughly translates to, "Τιτσιν Τιτσιν λουκάνικο και κομμάτια Ξεροτηανα, να Φασίν και να φιουσιν ".

   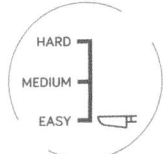 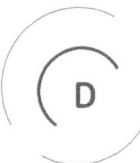 

Preparing the Dough

Dough mix

- 250g Plain flour
- 50g Vegan margarine
- 1 Tsp baking powder
- 120ml Almond, soy, or oat milk
- 50g Caster sugar
- 2 Tbsp sunflower oil for mix
- Neutral oil for frying, such as sunflower oil
- ½ Tsp salt

Syrup

- 1 Cup water
- 1 Cup sugar
- 1 Tsp rose water
- 50g Golden syrup
- 2 Whole cloves and a piece of lemon rind

Stir to dissolve the sugar. Then simmer for 8-10 minutes on a medium heat without stirring. Cool the syrup before you immerse the hot doughnuts, and then top as you please

Toppings

- Honey or golden syrup
- Sugar/icing sugar
- Chopped walnuts
- Ground cinnamon
- Orange or lemon zest

Cooking Method

1. Melt the butter over a low heat. Stir in 2 tbsp of oil and milk. Then, take off the heat

2. Mix the flour, baking powder, and salt in a bowl

3. Make a well in the centre of the flour. Add the milk mixture using a fork to combine the ingredients into a thick dough. You can use your hands, at this stage, to bring the mixture together and knead for a minute or two

4. Divide mixture into similar-size pieces. Then, roll into balls. Flatten each out slightly. Then, use your thumb to press out a hole in the centre, making a doughnut shape. Lightly flour your hands if the dough is sticking

5. Heat a deep saucepan on a medium-high heat. Add 2-3cm of oil, and heat. To check the oil is hot enough, drop a little dough into the oil. If it rises quickly to the top, the oil is hot enough

6. Gently place the doughnuts into the hot oil, and fry a few at a time, so as the temperature does not drop too much. The doughnuts should puff up nicely, when they meet the hot oil

7. Fry on each side for 2-3 minutes, or until beautifully golden brown. Then, place the cooked doughnuts on a plate, lined with a kitchen towel to absorb any excess oil

8. Repeat, until all the doughnuts are fried. Turn down heat if the doughnuts are becoming dark brown

9. Immerse each doughnut in the syrup

10. Transfer to a serving dish, and serve with any of the toppings you choose

> **Top Tip.**
> Mould the raw dough into balls, and flatten slightly without making a hole in centre. When fried and cooled, you can fill centres with jam, chocolate, or fruit purée.

Jellies

Μπανάνα
Ζελέ

Banana Jelly   Μπανάνα Ζελέ

Records show the cultivation of sugar in Cyprus since the 10th century. Cypriots have been busy finding uses for it ever since. Jelly and set chilled custards are really popular in countries which have a hot climate, as they are a light and cooling way to end a meal. After one too many times of having to decline a portion of mouthwatering and refreshing dessert, I endeavoured to make up a recipe, which did not include dairy. I developed these recipes from the Cypriot ingredients that I love, and have in my cupboard, and tested them on my family and friends. I hope you enjoy them.

Preparing the Jelly

Jelly

- 50g Cornflour
- 30g Sugar
- 120ml Greek banana cordial
- 1 Pint water

Syrup

- 4 Tbsp banana cordial
- 100ml Very cold water

Cooking Method

1. Pour some of the cold water with the cornflour into a saucepan. Use a balloon whisk to mix it into a smooth paste

2. Stir in the sugar and the remaining water. Then, put the pan on a medium heat. Whisk constantly until it bubbles and becomes translucent. Turn down heat and stir in 10g more of cold water, and turn off heat

3. Whisk in the banana cordial allocated to the jelly, and divide into four dishes or one larger one. Use a spatula to scrape all the jelly out of the pan. Then, refrigerate

4. After the jelly is completely set, mix the ingredients for the syrup, and spoon evenly onto the surface of each jelly. Serve

Footnote.
Complete the dish, including the layer of syrup, if refrigerating overnight, and cover the dish with cling film.

Top Tip.
Work very quickly when you take the jelly off the heat, as it sets very quickly.

Rose Cordial Jelly

Τριαντάφυλλο Ζελέ

A delicate and aromatic variation of a jelly flavour although not in a perfumed way.

Preparing the Jelly

Jelly

- 50g Cornflour
- 30g Sugar
- 120ml Greek rose cordial
- 1 Pint water
- 4 Tbsp Greek rose water

Syrup

- 4 Tbsp rose Cordial
- 1 Tsp rose water
- 100ml water

Cooking Method

1. Pour a little of the cold water into a saucepan, use a balloon whisk to mix them together into a smooth paste

2. Stir in the sugar and the remaining water and put the pan on a medium heat, whisk constantly until it bubbles and becomes translucent. Turn down heat and stir in 10g more of cold water and take off the heat

3. Whisk in the banana cordial allocated to the jelly and divide into four dishes or one larger one. Use a spatula to scrape all the jelly out of the pan. Refrigerate

4. When the jelly is completely set and cold. Combine the ingredients for the syrup and spoon evenly onto the surface of each jelly

Footnote.
Complete the dish including the layer of syrup if refrigerating overnight and cover the dish with cling film.

Top Tip.
Work very quickly when you take the jelly off the heat as it sets very quickly

Mosaic Jelly Μωσαϊκό Ζελέ

This is both a tasty and visual treat to make when you are having a get together and would like a crowd-pleasing colourful centrepiece. Made up of a red, yellow and white jellies, it resembles a mosaic pattern when finished, and hence called 'mosaic' jelly.

Cooking Method

1. Follow the directions for banana jelly and rose cordial jelly respectively. Moisten 2 loaf tins with cold water, and pour one jelly in to each. Set for 4-6 hrs. Cover each with cling film

2. Follow the directions for the 'Levantine Cream' of your choice (as featured on page 150)

3. Working quickly, turn out the banana jelly onto a plate. Cut the jelly into large cubes and place into a large glass serving dish which you have moistened with water. Then, repeat with the rose jelly

4. Stir the levantine custard and pour into the dish. Gently move the set cubes of jelly to evenly distribute through the dish. Refrigerate

5. Make a simple syrup of 1 cup water, 1 cup sugar, 1 whole spice clove, and 2 tbsp rose water. Bring to the boil and simmer for 8-10 minutes. Then, allow to cool

6. When the Jelly is completely set, spoon on the cold syrup, discarding the clove, and refrigerate for a further 30 minutes before serving straight from the dish

Top Tip.
Use a large jelly mould and make a stripy layered jelly. Simply make one flavour at a time. Allow each layer to set before pouring in the next. Repeat with as many layers as you like. Remember to moisten the mould first using a neutral cooking oil, and to cover the jelly with cling film. Place a serving plate over the mould, and then turn upside down to turn out the jelly.

Cakes

Ελιόπιτα

Eliopita Olive Bread Cake

Έλιοπιττα

It is common knowledge that Cypriots love olives - and I am no exception! There are many variations of eliopittes which means 'with olives' and traditionally they are made with sheets of pastry dough, which are spread with an olive tapenade, cut into squares, and rolled into individual crescent shapes. They are the number one fast fasting/vegan food, and are even more popular running up to Easter, when we fast for lent. Like brioche, this cake is savoury and ever so slightly sweet. However, they are unlike in texture. Although I love to cook, I really don't enjoy dough making by any method. My method, therefore ticks all the boxes, as I get that great olive pie 'hit' without the fuss of making dough or individual olive pies.

  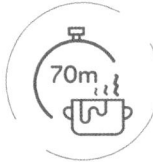 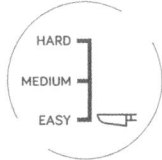  

Preparing the Cake

- 500g Self-raising flour
- 2 Heaped tsp of baking powder
- 250g Black olives, pitted and chopped (drain them if they are brined)
- 30g Fresh flat leaf parsley or coriander leaves. Rinse, pat dry, and chop
- 1 Onion, peeled, finely chopped or 3 spring onions, discard outer leaves, rise, dry and chop finely.
- 125ml Light olive oil

and
- 200ml Freshly-squeezed orange juice + 1 tbsp sugar

or
- 200ml Carbonated fizzy orange

and
- Zest and juice of one orange
- Add tap water to juice to make up to 200ml of liquid
- 1 Tbsp dried mint
- Pinch of salt
- 1 Tsp of olive oil for drizzling on top (optional)
- Sesame seeds for decoration (optional)

Cooking Method

1. Pre-heat your oven to 180°C/355°F
2. Grease and flour a 10" round spring-base cake tin. Then, cut greaseproof/baking parchment to line the base of your pan. Grease and flour the tin before you add the paper
3. Place the dried ingredients in a large mixing bowl, and mix with a wooden spoon
4. Place the wet ingredients (including the onions, olives and chopped herbs) in another bowl, and mix well
5. Then, make an indentation in the flour mix, pour in half the wet mixture, and incorporate it into the flour mix. Gently stir it well, then add the other half, and stir until well combined
6. Spoon your mixture into the cake tin. Flatten on the top and even out the mixture with a spatula. Then, drizzle with the 1 Tsp of olive oil, and evenly sprinkle over the sesame seeds
7. Place in a pre-heated fan oven for 70 minutes. Then, check it with a thin sharp knife; when inserted, it should come out clean. If not, continue to bake for a few more minutes. Your cake should be quite firm and have a light brown bread-like colour top
8. Remove your cake from the oven and allow it to rest for at least 15 minutes, before you turn it out. Refrigerate, once cooled

Serve with soups or stews. This is lovely cold in lunchboxes, and an ideal addition to any cheese board.

Footnote.
You will require 250g of olives. Check the drained weight of the product you are using.

Top Tip.
Bake in a lined and greased 3lb loaf tin, for loaf-shaped slices.

Φανούροπιτα

Saintly Vegan Cake

Φανούροπιτα

This aptly-named, sweet, demi-risen cake is made to celebrate the Annual Day of Saint Fanourios on 27th August, whose name means 'to reveal. We pray to this saint to help us find lost things, or to pray for something our hearts desire. This commemoration falls during a time of fasting for many Greek Orthodox practitioners, and yet, we manage to satisfy our sweet tooth in true Greek style with this cake. I came across a slice of this delicious, moist cake at a coffee morning in my aunt's courtyard – 'avli' in Cyprus many years ago. I tasted this cake after a Sunday service at church, where it had been taken to be 'blessed'. We commemorate the familial saints, after whom we are named on the respective days of the year, in which they fall. This is a special time for my family and I, as it also falls on the same weekend as my youngest son's Saints day of Saint Alexandros/Alexandria - on 30th August. Make this saintly vegan cake at any time you please, and say a little prayer. You never know - you may find what you are looking for.

   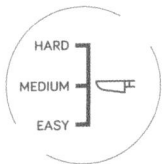 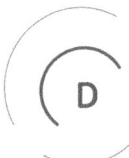 

Preparing the Cake

9"-10" inch round spring-base cake tin, greased and floured.
Use the same size cup to measure the ingredients.

- 500g of Self-raising flour, sieved
- 240ml Orange juice
- 200ml Vegetable oil or light olive oil
- 210g Sugar
- 65g Chopped walnuts
- 1 Tsp ground cinnamon
- 2 Level tsp baking powder
- 1 Tsp vanilla extract
- 1 Tbsp brandy or ¼ tsp ground cloves
- Zest from one orange

Cooking Method

1. Preheat fan oven to 170 degrees C
2. Grease, flour, and line your tin, before you begin the batter
3. In a mixing bowl, combine the brandy, sugar, oil, orange zest, and the orange juice, until the sugar dissolves completely
4. Combine all of the dry ingredients in a separate mixing bowl
5. Make a well in the centre of the flour, and use a wooden spoon to mix the ingredients together. Do not overwork the batter
6. Stir in the nuts when you have finished
7. Pour the batter into the cake tin, using the spatula to scrape out the contents of the bowl. Spread the mixture evenly into the pan, and pat down with the spatula, as this batter is a little more dense than a usual cake batter
8. Bake in the oven for 60-65 minutes, or until a knife comes out clean, when you pierce the cake. Let the cake rest, out of the oven, for at least 10 minutes, before you try to turn out

Footnote.
You may make this without nuts, and the recipe remains the same.
If desired, you may sprinkle the cooled cake with icing sugar.

Troubleshooting
- As with all cakes, do not open oven door.
- Level the baking powder.
- Do not underbake.
- Do not let the cake batter stand too long before baking.

Top Tip.
When you are making batter, if you feel it is a little bit on the dense side, add 10ml or more orange juice.

Κέικ
Νηστίσιμο

Fruity Vegan Cake   Κέικ Νηστίσιμο

This sweet, risen fruit cake is a firm favourite. In light of the fact that this recipe does not contain eggs or dairy, it is unbelievably light, fruity, and flavourful. This recipe came about, whilst I practised many a Christmas cake and puddings. I much prefer this lighter version, which I make to replace these, and decorate according to the occasion. More often than not I serve it naked, as soon as it has cooled, with a cup of Greek coffee. The technique of floating fruit evaded me so many times, that I nearly gave up making it altogether. Trial and a great deal of error later taught me to lightly flour the fruit, before adding it to the batter at the last minute, seems to do the trick. Great for a coffee morning with friends, and as a healthier sweet addition for your packed lunches, this recipe is a super alternative to vegan cake recipes which contain nuts.

  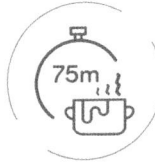 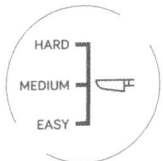  

Preparing the Cake

9"-10" inch round spring-base cake tin or a bundt tin

- 500g Self-raising flour, sieved
- 210g Sugar
- 150g Mixed dried fruit, currants, sultanas, or raisins (any ratio)
- 200ml Vegetable oil
- 2 Level tbsp baking powder
- 40ml Brandy
- 370ml Orange juice
- Zest from one orange
- ½ Tsp ground cinnamon
- 1 Tsp vanilla extract

Cooking Method

1. Preheat the fan oven to 165 degrees C
2. Beat the oil, sugar, orange zest, and ¼ of the orange juice, until the sugar has dissolved, and the mixture is very well combined
3. In a separate mixing bowl, use a hand balloon whisk to mix the remaining orange juice, the brandy, baking powder, ground cinnamon, ground cloves, and orange zest, until they are combined and begins to froth
4. Use a spatula to scrape out all the baking powder mixture, and combine the contents of both bowls thoroughly
5. Stir in the sieved flour with a spatula. Try not to overwork the batter
6. Grease and flour the cake tin
7. Put the mixed fruit in a bowl, and lightly sprinkle with flour. Add the floured fruit to the batter, without adding more flour. Stir just enough to distribute the fruit
8. Pour the batter into the tin, using the spatula to scrape out the bowl and even the batter out
9. Bake in the oven for 70-75 minutes, or until a sharp knife comes out clean, when you pierce the cake. Let the cake rest, out of the oven, for at least 10 minutes, before trying to turn out

Decorate with a dusting of icing sugar, or glaze with a little marmalade, when the cake is completely cool.

Footnote.
Do not open the oven door for the first 50 minutes. Do not underbake. Push any fruit, which are peeping out, back into the batter with a knife before baking.

Top Tip.
Make this in a greased, floured, 3lb loaf tin with a lined base, if you would like to cut it into slices more easily.

Κέικ με Ινδοκάρυδο

Alexander the Great Coconut Cake

Κέικ με Ινδοκαρυδο

Named after one of my children, as it is their favourite cake recipe, this was one of the first cakes I ever baked. It now seems a lifetime ago. A similar recipe was passed down to me from a great aunt years ago. For the sake of posterity, and because it so delicious, it has to be recorded for my heirs. Cypriots considered coconuts to be a rare and extravagant ingredient - as perhaps a great many of us did. As this delicately-flavoured, tropical fruit was very hard to come by, and few could afford it, it makes this recipe even more special. These days, however, I have replaced my aunts choice of decoration - glaze cherries with desiccated coconut. Even though coconut and its products are not as difficult or as expensive to source today, this cake tastes just as special now, as the first time I made it. In true Greek fashion, a fluffy, risen cake is doused with a delicately-aromatic sweet syrup.

   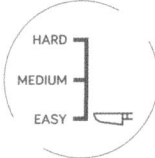 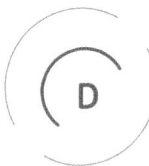 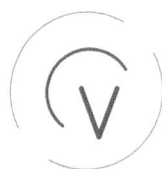

Preparing the Cake

Cake Batter

- 410ml Vegetable or sunflower oil
- 210g Sugar
- 320g Self-raising flour
- 3 Tsp baking powder
- 5 Eggs
- 150g Dessicated coconut
- 120ml Milk
- 2 Tbsp brandy or 1 tsp vanilla extract

Syrup

- 200g Sugar
- 220ml Water
- 5 Whole clove spice
- 1 Small stick cassia bark
- 1 Tbsp rose water

Decoration

- 1-2 Tbsp desiccated coconut

Cooking Method

You will need an 11" bundt cake tin (the one with the hole) or a 10" springform cake tin, greased and floured. Do not skip this step, as it will enable your cake to be released from the tin freely.

1. Preheat fan oven to 175 degrees C
2. Grease, flour, and line your tin
3. Measure all your ingredients before you begin
4. Pour the milk into a bowl. Stir in the coconut, and allow it to be absorbed the liquid
5. Make the syrup by adding all the ingredients to a saucepan. Stir until the sugar is dissolved. Put on a medium heat, bring to the boil, turn down heat to low, set a timer, and then gently simmer for 8 minutes without stirring. When timer is finished, take off heat and allow to cool
6. In two bowls, separate the egg yolks from the egg whites. Using a hand whisk, beat the egg whites, until light and fluffy and have increased in volume and formed soft peaks
7. Beat the egg yolks with the remaining wet ingredients, and add the sugar to the egg yolks. Continue to beat with a hand whisk, until the mixture is light, the sugar has dissolved, and the mixture is fluffy and pale in colour
8. Follow with the soaked coconut and all the milk. Stir to mix
9. Sieve the flour into another bowl, and then add the baking powder and cinammon
10. Make a well in the centre of the flour and add the wet ingredients. Mix until all the ingredients are just combined. Do not over mix as the flour will stiffen and give you a dense cake
11. Using a spatula, stir the egg whites in 1/3 - at a time, until all the egg whites are incorporated
12. Pour mixture into tin. Use a spatula to smooth and even out the cake batter. If using a bundt tin, rotate it, as you pour, so that the mixture goes in evenly
13. Bake in the oven for 50-55 minutes, or until a knife comes out clean, when you pierce cake. If not, bake a little longer
14. Let the cake stand for 15 minutes, before you turn out
15. Turn cake out on to a serving dish. Pour the cooled syrup over the sponge - 1/3 at a time, in 5-minute intervals. Discard clove and cassia bark. Sprinkle with desiccated coconut to decorate

---

Top Tip.
Once baked, go round the sides of the tin with a thin plastic knife or small flat spatula. Then, to turn out of a bundt tin, take a large plate, and place it over the cake tin. Holding firmly with both hands, turn it over, put it down, remove the tin, and place cake stand over cake, and carefully turn it the right way up.

Footnote.
You can replace the rose water with orange rind if you like. Add cold syrup to warm cake, or vice versa.

Μπανάνα και Σοκολάτα Κέικ Ηπατισμο

Banana Chocolate Loaf Cake

Μπανάνα και Σοκολάτα Κέικ Νηστίσιμο

This cake incorporates two much-loved ingredients - banana and chocolate, which are a blissful combination. This recipe benefits greatly utilising the overripe bananas, that are often left hanging on trees, and then later discarded. The idea for this recipe came when my granddaughter was born. I developed it by replacing the sugar with honey, and then, further still, by removing dairy and eggs completely. I must confess that the chocolate chips where a later addition, as my granddaughter grew old enough to be allowed a little treat. This is a great recipe for children to make under adult supervision.

   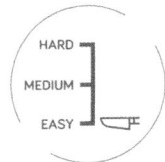  

Preparing the Cake

You will need a 2lb loaf tin, greased and floured, or lined with baking parchment, or a cake tin liner.

- 350g Overripe bananas for mixture. Also, one whole banana, sliced - to decorate. Once sliced, brush lightly with any citrus juice, such as lemon, pineapple, or orange juice to prevent browning
- 150ml Vegetable, sunflower, or light olive oil
- 150g Honey or golden syrup
- 300g Self-raising flour
- 100g Chocolate chips of your choice (or chop a bar of chocolate into small, chunky pieces instead)
- 1 Heaped tsp baking powder
- ½ Tsp bicarbonate of soda (for baking)

and

- 1 Tbsp ground cinammon

or

- 1 Tsp vanilla extract or both

and

- Pinch of salt (omit if baking for young children)

Glaze

- 3 Tbsp marmalade
- 1 Tsp water

Cooking Method

1. Preheat a fan oven to 170 degrees C
2. Add the flour through a sieve into a large bowl. Then, add the bicarbonate of soda, baking powder, cinnamon and a pinch of salt. Mix until all the ingredients are well combined
3. In a separate bowl, mash 350g (roughly 3-4) overripe bananas. Stir in the oil, vanilla extract, and honey, and mix well. Beat the flour into the banana mixture
4. Stir in the chocolate chips. Stir them into the mixture well
5. Pour the batter into the tin. Level the mixture out with the back of a spoon, and allow it to rest for 5 minutes before placing in the oven
6. When the batter has rested, slice the remaining banana lengthwise into it, and then place the slices on top of the batter down the middle of the tin. This decorates the cake, so take as much care as you would like with this step
7. Gently warm the marmalade with the water, and then leave to one side
8. Bake the banana cake until well risen, and until a skewer comes out clean from centre of cake. This is one cake that can be ever so slightly over baked. Remove from oven, and when the cake is cool, brush with the marmalade glaze. Remember to allow at least 10 minutes resting time before you turn out the cake

Footnote.
Perfect for lunchboxes. Lasts for up to 4 days in an airtight container. Keep in the fridge.

Top Tip.
Add 3 tbsp of cocoa powder to the batter mix to make this a double chocolate cake.

Chocolate Duchess   Δούκισσα

'Chocolate Duchess' is similar to a cake popularly known as a 'batik cake'. It is a method which involves little or no cooking. Chocolate was a luxury item in Cyprus, as it was very hard to store in such a hot climate, and manufacturers found it very difficult to stabilise. We 'Gringlish' maintain that Cypriot chocolate tastes completely different to that found in the UK. It is customary for us, as guests, to take a dish of something sweet - 'Γλυκη'. It is deemed very inappropriate if we turn up empty handed. When it is the turn of the hosts to visit, the favour/dish is returned in full. The 'Duchess' is a coveted timeless chocolate dessert, which is formed in a loaf tin and sliced. It is hugely popular and is among a long list of sweet treats given as 'favours' at celebrations such as christenings and weddings. In fact, 'The Duchess' was my daughters 'favour' of choice at her own engagement. Slices are wrapped individually in cellophane or bright foils, that tie in with the chosen colour scheme of the celebration, and given to each guest.

Preparing the Duchess

You will need a 2lb loaf tin.

- 450g Rich tea or morning coffee biscuits
- 60g Sugar
- 80g Cocoa powder
- 150g Water
- 35g Butter, margarine, or vegan alternative
- 1 Tbsp vanilla extract
- 2 Tsp brandy, brandy liqueur, honey, or golden syrup

or

- 2 Tsp of the sweet syrup from a jar of sweet fruit preserve, such as the traditional preserves you may have from your holidays abroad, known as "Γλυκό"

Cooking Method

1. Add all the ingredients to a saucepan. Stir over a medium heat until the sugar is dissolved and the ingredients have melted and combined well. Do not simmer. Just warm through, then take off heat, and put to one side to cool

2. Grease and line your loaf tin on both sides with a double amount of cling film - allowing it to overhang generously on all sides. You may use baking parchment if you prefer

3. Place biscuits in a large zip lock or tie handle bag, and use a rolling pin to break each biscuit into a few pieces. You may break the biscuits by hand if you prefer. You are looking for small pieces of biscuit, not gravel or sand, as you would use in a cheesecake

4. Put the broken biscuits in to a mixing bowl, and repeat until all the biscuits are broken

5. Reserve 20-30g of chocolate mixture.

6. Stir the chocolate well, and, if it has cooled to room temperature, add biscuit to the pan. Stir gently with a spatula until all the biscuits are all completely coated with the chocolate

7. Pour the reserved chocolate into the base of the lined tin. Cover the base evenly

8. Carefully spoon the mixture into the loaf tin. Then, scrape the pan out with the spatula and pat down the mixture right into the corners. Pour any remaining chocolate evenly over the biscuit, and carefully gather the cling film, covering the surface completely. Firmly pat the mixture down with the palm of your hand

9. Refrigerate for 6-8 hrs before turning out. It then needs to be stored in the fridge

---

Top Tip.
Slice and wrap the individual portions in pretty paper and ribbon and give as gifts.

Footnote.
Taste the chocolate mixture before mixing with biscuits, as you may prefer it to taste sweeter.

Παγωτό
και
Σορμπέ

Ice Cream & Sorbets

Ice Cream & Sorbets

Mastiha, Rose, Banana, Coconut, and Chocolate flavoured Ice Cream Sorbets

I am a firm believer that if your main ingredient or procedure in a dish incorporates water, whether it be boiling vegetables, cooking rice, or making iced desserts, then your dish will not taste of anything much. Vegan ice cream recipes are tricky, as you omit the dairy and eggs, which make them tasty, creamy, and smooth. You then replace them with water and sugar, the result of which can be a sugar-laden, tasteless ice cube. When experimenting with ingredients and recipes, I replaced the dairy and water with a variety of Mother Nature's wealth of coconut products.The first attempt was good, but not good enough; the second - great, but not quite there; the third was superb, even if I say so myself. I have included those recipes with all the guesswork, and trials and errors removed. The thread of coconut that runs through each recipe adds a luscious, yet subtle flavour, that pairs with the other ingredients perfectly. I am really proud of these sorbet recipes as they have managed to please the very cultured and experienced palettes of my family. Therefore, I hope that you enjoy them too, but, if you still need convincing, taking into account the enticing flavours, I have included instructions for those who do not have an ice cream churn. The Cypriots take their ice cream very seriously. They will have an ice cream cone with as many as 8-10 different flavours. It is called 'thiafora', which means an assortment. I recommend you make all these flavours and as the Greeks do have a little of each in one serving.

Top Tip.
Use a round-shaped container with a lid to make and store the sorbets, if you can - especially those made without the use of an ice cream churn. It makes the surface area smaller and helps to minimise ice crystals.

Coconut Iced Cream Sorbet

Ινδοκαρυδο Σορμπέ

     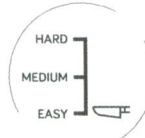 

Preparing the Sorbet

- 50g Desiccated coconut
- 200ml Coconut water (unsweetened)
- 15ml Rose water
- 400ml Tinned coconut milk
- 200g Sugar

Cooking Method

1. Soak the desiccated coconut with the coconut water for 30 minutes

2. Pour the coconut water into a saucepan over a sieve to catch the desiccated coconut. Pat down with the back of a spoon to drain. Put the sieve it to one side, add the sugar, stir to dissolve, and bring to the boil. Turn down heat and simmer without stirring for 6-8 minutes. Take off the heat and transfer to another container to cool for 1 hour

3. Using an electric hand whisk, beat the rose water into the coconut water mixture for 1-2 minutes, until it is well combined

4. Add the coconut milk to the coconut water and whisk for 3-4 minutes until the ingredients are a little aerated

5. Pour into an airtight container with a lid and place in the freezer for 1 hour

6. Remove from freezer and fork through the sorbet to prevent ice crystals. Then, place back in the freezer

7. Repeat step 6 twice more. Keep in freezer for a further 2-3 hours. Before serving, transfer to the fridge for 15 minutes to make scooping easier

Mastiha Iced Cream Sorbet

Μαστίχα Σορμπέ

The mere mention of the unique flavour of this ice cream transports my family and I back to our favourite ice cream parlour situated in a popular tourist village in Cyprus which makes the most heavenly ices, sorbets and frozen yoghurts. This flavour is unique to Cyprus although some Greek islands have a variation of this called 'Kaimaki'. Changes of late in familial diets and preferences caused me to take apart the traditional ice cream recipe that we loved and to substitute the banned ingredients using different elements whilst at the same time preserving the mastiha essence of the ice cream that we adore. This is a delicious hybrid of ice cream crossed with sorbet that manages to satiate even the most ardent mastiha ice cream fans.

    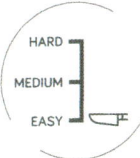 

Preparing the Sorbet

- 14 Chios mastic pieces + 1 Tbsp sugar for grinding
- 400ml Coconut milk
- 200g Sugar
- 200ml Coconut water

Cooking Method

1. Add the coconut water to a saucepan on a medium heat. Stir in the sugar until it dissolves, and allow to simmer for 5-6 minutes without stirring. Take off the heat, pour into a bowl, and allow to cool for 2-3 hrs in the fridge

2. Put 5g sugar and the mastic resin in a pestle and mortar, and grind the mastic resin until it is a coarse powder

3. Add the coconut milk to the cooled syrup and whisk for 3-5 minutes, until both are really well combined and the mix is lightly aerated

4. Whisk in the ground mastic resin

5. Pour into an ice cream maker and churn until it becomes a sorbet. Then, transfer to an airtight container with a lid and freeze. If you do not have an ice cream maker pour the finished sorbet mix into an airtight container, and freeze for 30 minutes. Then, fork through the sorbet to prevent ice crystals

6. Repeat step 5 twice more, if you do not have an ice cream churner, return to freezer for a further 3-4 hours or overnight. Before serving, transfer to the fridge for 15 minutes to make scooping easier

Rose Flavour Iced Cream Sorbet

Τριαντάφυλλο Σορμπέ

Rose cordial has been made in Cyprus for years and is a very special product. This particular flavour tastes great spooned on to the Mahalepi recipe included, as featured on page 148 in this cookbook, instead of the syrup.

   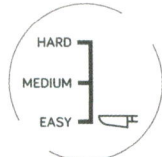 

Preparing the Sorbet

- 200ml Rose cordial
- 15ml Rose water
- 20ml Coconut milk
- 280ml Coconut water
- 200g Sugar
- ½ Whole lemon, juiced

Cooking Method

1. Dissolve the sugar and the coconut water in a saucepan. Then, place on a medium heat and bring to the boil. Turn down heat, simmer for 6-8 minutes without stirring. Take off the heat. Stir in the lemon juice

2. Add the rose cordial, rose water, and coconut milk to a big jug. Stir until all the ingredients are well blended. Combine this mixture with the syrup blend

3. Pour into an ice cream churn until it becomes a sorbet. Then, transfer to an airtight container with a lid and freeze. If you do not have an ice cream churn, transfer to an airtight container with a lid, and freeze for 1 hour. Then, remove from freezer, fork through to prevent ice crystals from forming, and then place back in freezer

4. Repeat step 3 twice more. Freeze for 4-5 hours or overnight

5. Transfer to the fridge 15 minutes before serving to make scooping easier

Chocolate Sorbet

Σοκολάτα Σορμπέ

This dairy-free, yet smooth and creamy chocolate sorbet flavour has long since been one of my must haves in my preferential trio of ice cream sundae flavours.

Preparing the Sorbet

- 200g Sugar
- 50g Cocoa powder
- 50g 70% Dark chocolate, finely chopped
- 1 Tsp vanilla extract
- 600ml Coconut water

Cooking Method

1. Tip the sugar into a bowl, sift in the cocoa and stir. Bring the coconut water to the boil in a medium saucepan. Whisk in the sugar and cocoa powder and return to a gentle simmer. Simmer, uncovered, for 5 mins, whisking occasionally. Remove from the heat and stir in the chocolate and vanilla until the chocolate has melted

2. Cool the mixture, then put in an ice cream churn until it becomes a sorbet, then transfer to an airtight container with a lid and freeze or if you do not have an ice cream churner beat with a hand whisk until it becomes aerated then transfer to airtight container with a lid and cool in fridge for 2-3 hours

3. Whisk to prevent ice crystals forming, freeze and repeat step 2 two more times

4. Place in freezer until completely frozen

5. Before serving, transfer to the fridge for 15 minutes to make scooping easier

Banana Iced Cream Sorbet

Μπανάνα Σορμπέ

The traditional banana cordial makes this such a soft-textured and very creamy sorbet. It is 'lip smackingly' good - and no cooking required. There are 4 ingredients, 5 steps - it's really that simple!

Preparing the Sorbet

- 150ml Coconut water
- 150ml Coconut milk
- 200ml Greek banana cordial
- 30g Sugar

Cooking Method

1. Whisk the sugar with the coconut water until completely dissolved

2. Whisk in the coconut milk for 3-4 minutes

3. Whisk in the banana cordial for a further 1-2 minutes. Then, pour into an ice cream churn until it becomes a sorbet. Afterwards, transfer to an airtight container with a lid, and freeze. If you don't have an ice cream churner, please proceed to next step

4. Pour into an airtight container with lid, and freeze for one hour. Remove from freezer and fork through to prevent ice crystals from forming. Then, place back in freezer

5. Repeat step 4 twice more, and then place back in freezer for 4-5 hours or until frozen

6. Place in fridge 15 minutes before serving to make scooping easier

Footnote.
30g of sugar is not a typo, the banana cordial also contains sugar.

TIPS THRIFT, TRICKS & TACTICS

What has developed into a lifetime in the food industry, and cooking and baking for family and friends, has given me an abundance of knowledge. This has been enhanced by my love for cooking, as well as an innate curiosity of all ingredients and cuisines. My aim was to record that experience for my family. The thought of future generations having tips, guidance and the know how is very pleasing to me. It would fill me with great joy, if they put into practise some essential life skills, by enjoying the fruits of my labour, without doing a lot of the groundwork. Life is too short to spend life on the little things, which, unfortunately, make a big difference. I start this section with a humble recommendation, meals should be about fun, family, and not simply about food. This should take place at least once a week - any day that suits you. Eat a homemade meal together as a family - it can be as simple as a bowl of pasta, or even your special breakfast of choice, taken at the time you please. You will find that scheduling a sit-down meal, TV off or muted in the background, is a great way to bond as a family - even if your family consists of you and one other. It is a necessary social ability to pass on to your children, which will help keep them grounded and give them lasting memories. With the passing of time, no one will notice that the TV is not the focal point. Generations of hard-working Cypriots will all tell you the same thing - at least once a week we eat together as a family.

Leading on with what may seem like an obvious tip, I suggest that you read through all new recipes twice before you start to cook. In this way, you can build a picture in your mind of how best to begin, so that you can ensure you have all the utensils, pans, and ingredients that are required. Always use a bigger pan than you think you will need. This is far easier and safer than transferring hot food to a larger pan. Do not use damp/wet oven gloves or cloths to handle hot pans and dishes, as this can cause serious burns.

Clean down all surfaces before preparing meals, and wash your hands thoroughly before and after handling raw and cooked food. Wear gloves, if possible, to handle high risk foods such as raw meat, poultry, and fish.
Disinfect or bleach the sink regularly, After each time you prepare raw meat and seafood products, ensure you completely rinse away all traces of any cleaning products after use. Rinse all ingredients prior to use. This extends to pre-packaged washed salads, fruit, and vegetables.

Plan your meals ahead as much as possible. This saves time and food waste.
Clean out your fridge before you go food shopping. It's far easier to clean an empty fridge, and also gives the opportunity to double check items you need to purchase.
Keep a list of products/ingredients you require, or have run out of, as you go along. You can refer to this list quickly when you go shopping.

I believe that there are 10 items or less required in your store cupboard to be able to rustle up a quick meal. These are as follows. Extra virgin olive oil, light olive oil, fresh onion, whole lemon, a pack of dry pasta or rice, tinned chopped tomatoes or tomato pasatta, stock cubes, frozen peas, a dry herb such as oregano or basil, and perhaps a piece of halloumi cheese or vegan alternative.

If you are short of time, batch prepare and cook as much as possible in advance. Refrigerate vegetables, washed salad and fruit, ready to be used.

Refrigerate cooked leftovers, as soon as they are cool, as this prolongs the time they can be safely eaten.

Defrost all food completely prior to consumption. The best way to defrost food safely is to place it in the fridge and allow it to thaw out overnight.

Reheat food thoroughly prior to consumption. This means the core must reach the temperature of 75 degrees C. If you are reheating food in a microwave, stir the dish half way through cooking time, wherever possible, and then continue to heat. If you are unable to stir the dish, allow food to stand for two minutes halfway through cooking time, then continue to heat.

Variety is not only the 'spice of life', but the key to achieving a nutritionally-balanced diet, which is essential for good health. All food varies greatly in composition and nutritional value. The simplest way to attain a well-balanced diet, with the best health benefits, is to include many different coloured ingredients, and vary them as much and often as possible. This should be combined with the addition of exercise, which can be as simple as running the vacuum round or going up and down the stairs a few times a day.

Quality of sleep is also essential for good health. If you find that you are not getting a good night's sleep, get to the bottom of why, and try to resolve it. There are many reasons for poor quality sleep. This can be as simple as your room being too hot or cold. Alternatively, it could be down to more complex reasons, underlying health issues, or stress and anxiety, for which you should ask for help. Start with your GP, or go online for self-help groups specific to your problem. Controversially, sleep in the spare room or on the sofa bed one or two nights a week, if you are coupled with a restless partner, one that snores, or one that requires some type of noise emitting machine attached to them. These are all an antithesis to a good night's sleep.

Swap white for brown/wholemeal, where possible it is a simple swap, which offers far better nutritional benefits. I follow this basic guideline with the exception of rice and orzo pasta. In my view, brown rice has far too many phytates or anti-nutrients, and in some cases, high levels of arsenic. It is more difficult to digest and longer to cook, which far outweighs any benefits, as white rice on the whole is enriched by the manufacturers and we are able to add nutritious stock and other ingredients to it during the cooking process.

Rice is a high-risk food, whether uncooked or cooked. Store dry rice in its original packaging in a cool dark place. Rinse raw rice before using. Cook thoroughly and consume on the same day.

Use clean utensils to dip into pickles, jams, sauces, preserves, and sugar etc. Do not double dip. This will minimise the risk of introducing bacteria to the product and will prolong it's freshness and taste.

Preheat pans prior to adding oil. Add the oil only when you are ready to cook. It is far safer, as you will find that some eventuality will distract you, whilst you have a pan of hot oil on the heat.

To rid your hands of the smell of garlic and raw fish after handling them, wash your hands, along with your regular hand wash in cold water. Washing with warm/hot water sets the odour into your pores. If you find that the smell continues to linger, moisturise your hands with your favourite moisturiser or olive oil. Wait 10-15 minutes, then wash your hands with warm water and soap. It always does the trick for me!

Fussy eaters.

Take children shopping from a young age and allow them to choose a different piece of fresh fruit, vegetable, or salad each time you shop. Purchase their choice and then take it home, and help them to prepare it. Introduce them to a varied diet from the moment you wean them, and their range of food will grow with them. Allow them to help you prepare meals, as this will accustom them to different ingredients, and it will encourage them to try new flavours. Find your nearest farms and research what they have on offer, such as live chickens, which lay eggs, fruit picking, or even crop cutting. Take away whatever you can to then eat at home.

Together with your children, sow edible herbs in planters, or a little pot of mint. Infuse the leaves in warm water, add some honey, and let them taste the produce they have grown.

Cook food in advance as much as possible. Make it the 'norm' that they will have a meal ready. I have found that, if food is at hand, when children are hungry, or when they come in from school, work or play, that they are more open to trying new dishes. Stand your ground and do not allow choice or treats until after meal times.

Sourcing ingredients

Our supermarkets have vastly improved the range of 'foreign produce' available to purchase, and I find that most items are easily available. If you are experiencing difficulty finding some ingredients, contact your local Greek Orthodox Church. You can do this by calling the listed telephone number or by popping into your local Greek Church on a Sunday. On the whole, Greeks are generally philanthropic, and will definitely steer you in the right direction. Often, our churches also house our community centres and Saturday school. Failing this, try the researching on the internet.

Fresh is best, don't waste the rest.

With so much food going to waste, I am definitely from the school of thought that believes that tackling unnecessary food waste is the responsibility of all of us. We can all start reducing our carbon footprint at home by checking everything before we throw it away. With the exception of meat, shellfish, fish, and food labelled 'use by', which is for our safety, do not discard whole bags of food if one or two pieces are past their best. Throw the offending items away and use the rest. Store food correctly, and according to the manufacturers' instructions, to prolong freshness and quality. Remember to label and date all products, before you freeze them.

Tomatoes, that seem over ripe and soft, are perfect for pasta sauces or for cooking as in dishes like 'yiachni'. They are also lovely, roughly chopped and gently sautéed until soft, in light olive oil then add a lightly beaten egg or two, season and scramble, serve on seeded toast with smashed avocado. This is great post-workout dish or an easy brunch meal. To remove the skin of the tomatoes, score an 'x' into the base of each tomato - do not cut into flesh. Then, immerse in boiling hot water, until the skin begins to peel back, remove one at a time from water, and peel off the skin with a knife. Decant any surplus pasatta or tinned tomatoes into an airtight container with a lid, and they will keep for up to three days. Record the weight, date, and product, on a freezer bag and freeze. Or, you could make the speedy tomato and basil sauce for pizzas or pasta.

With lettuce and leafy salads, which are whole and on the stalk, and just beginning to spoil, just discard the soft and brown outer layers, rinse, and use as required. Pre-packaged salads, that have spoiled, should always be discarded. Fresh herbs such as parsley, coriander, and chillies all freeze well. Finely chop and freeze.

Eggs

Freshly-laid eggs are safe to eat for up to 28 days. If your eggs are within their 'best before date', crack them individually into greased cupcake tins, and freeze. They will last for up to 4 months. Or, use up eggs by making an omelette, pancakes, muffins, or bake a cake. Alternatively, hard boiled eggs, and keep them in the fridge ready to be used for sandwiches or as a quick low fat snack. If you are unsure when raw eggs are suitable to eat, immerse, one at a time, in a glass or jugful of cold water. Eggs that sink are still fresh; eggs that sink but tilt to one side are still safe to eat; discard any eggs that float.

Uncooked dry pasta, legumes, rice, pulses, and beans, that have been stored correctly in a cool, dark, and dry place should be safe to eat up to 6 months after their 'best before date' if they are clear of mould, microbes and the integrity of the product is intact.

Drain raw unused soaked legumes such Cannellini beans and black-eyed beans of the soaking water and store in fridge for up to 3 days or in the freezer for up to 1 month. This is a great way to prevent spoiling, but you will have pre-soaked beans when you need them. Defrost thoroughly before use, and cook as the recipe states.

Dried Herbs & Spices

These have a tendency to lose their potency - especially if they are past their 'sell by' date. You may follow the right recipe and find that the finished dish does not taste quite as it should. Purchase the smallest quantities available and store them in a cool dark place, in airtight containers. If you must decant them, ensure they are clearly labelled, along with the date. I always opt to purchase from Asian/Mediterranean sources, as, in my view, their herbs and spices are far superior in both taste and freshness. In most cases, spices require some moisture and warming to release their flavour, oils, and aroma, and are usually added at the beginning of cooking. In contrast, fresh herbs should be added as late as possible to balance the flavour of a dish, and do not require a lot of cooking. Using herbs and spices to flavour food, is also a great way to enhance a dish, whilst reducing the amount of salt. In respect of pepper, it should be freshly ground into cooking. This is, with the exception for white pepper, which should be treated as a spice and warmed through.

Bread

Freeze sliced bread when fresh. Defrost the amount required in an airtight container or toast straight from the freezer. You can also slice whole loaves of bread, and then freeze. Uncut stale bread can be used to make breadcrumbs, which can then be frozen. Stale bread, croissants, and brioche, which are free of mould, are perfect for bread and butter puddings. Finally, if none of the above appeal to you, feed the birds in your garden or in the local park. They can safely eat stale bread, but, in the same way as us, do not feed them mouldy bread.

Fruit

Make a fruit salad with any fruit you have leftover or fruit that is about to spoil, except soft berries and bananas. Simply rinse, peel, and discard pips and seeds. Then, chop into bite-sized pieces. Add a splash of any fresh fruit juice, and a drop of lemon to stop it browning. Finally, place in the fridge in an airtight container or eat as a dessert with a spoonful of plain yoghurt or cream, and a drizzle of honey or golden syrup. Freeze soft fruit. Berries and bananas are especially good for smoothies. Defrost and add to porridge for breakfast, or scoop onto plain ice cream. They work well on pancakes too. You can also freeze all berries and lemon slices individually, into ice cube trays, and use them as ice for drinks or cocktails.

Simmer down any combination of fruit, with a little sugar and water, to make a fruit purée. This is a wholesome option for babies' and toddlers' desserts, as long as they remain sugar free. You can also make a crumble or a pie.
Fruit, such as banana, apples, pears, pineapple, mango, grapes and berries etc, can be baked in a dry oven, on a really low heat at about 90 degrees C. Stirring every 30 minutes or so, bake until the fruit is dry and chewy. When you are happy with the texture of the fruit turn off oven. Then, leave fruit in oven, with door open, for a further 20 minutes. Finally, close oven door, with the fruit inside, and leave for a few hours or overnight. Remember to peel thick-skinned fruit, such as mango. Oven-dried fruit is a healthy snack in lunchboxes and delicious when added to your cereal or porridge. All fruit is suitable for smoothies and shakes.

Vegetables and Salads

As there is such an abundant list of vegetables and salad ingredients, I will not attempt to instruct you on the best way to use each of them. Try to to use as diverse a range as possible. Regularly mixing things up will, in itself, give your tastebuds a treat. This can be achieved by adopting little tweaks to the preparation and cooking of vegetables and salads such as layering your ingredients with flavour, a simple dressing comprising of a pinch of salt, squirt of lemon juice and some extra virgin olive oil will transform a salad from boring to appetising. Adding a little crushed stock into vegetables, when you are cooking them, can make them taste far more flavourful and appetising. My tip is to always cook vegetables with sugars, stock, alcohol, or juice, as opposed to just water. If baking vegetables in the oven, do not forget to drizzle them with olive oil, a pinch of salt, and freshly ground pepper. Bake sweet potatoes in an ovenproof dish, along with some water, stock, and light olive oil for magnificent results.

Cabbage, kale, carrot, greens, spinach, watercress, lettuce, celery, bok choy, and avocado are good for smoothies and shakes. Avocado is also perfect used for guacamole, a dip for tortilla, crudités, or simply smashed with a fork on toast. Add a drop of lemon juice to maintain its colour, if storing as a dip in the fridge

Make a vegetable soup, by simply following the basic recipe in this book, and then adding any leftover vegetables you have. Discard only the fibrous outer leaves of vegetables, such as cauliflower. The inner leaves are just as edible and nutritious.

Freeze leftover bits and pieces of cheese. Grate them to use in cheese or béchamel sauce, and pour over cooked broccoli, cauliflower, or potato gratin. You can also grate frozen cheese straight onto pasta.

Freeze any leftover wine from opened bottles into ice cube or freezer bags. Simply pop them out, as you need them in cooking.

Juice lemons and store the liquid in the fridge for up to 3 days. Alternatively, freeze for up to one month, or pop them in your cutlery tray or top shelf of your dishwasher to act as an anti bacterial and to eliminate odours. Sliced lemon is also great in warm water. Honey or golden syrup or in cold water also provides a refreshing zing.

Allergies and Food intolerances

Read the ingredients list on the packaging carefully - especially on products, with which you are not familiar. Do not use ingredients you are unsure of. I have found that there is a great deal of confusion in respect of allergies, as opposed to intolerances. There are no exceptions to safety. If you suffer from an allergy then you must refrain from ingesting or coming into contact with the offending product completely.

Disclaimer.
The oven temperatures and timings I have provided are based on
the use of a fan oven and a gas hob. Please adjust temeratures and
timings acording to your respective appliances.

Notes

Meze
Index

Meze - 'Μεζέ' or 'Mezethes' - 'Μεζέδες' in plural, are the Greek equivalent of a cheese and wine party, but with Greek bells and whistles. Greeks consider it poor form to drink without some sort of food as an accompaniment. This benefits both mind and stomach. Meze is a languorous experience, which should be delivered in a laid-back and convivial style, encompassing all age groups and dietary requirements. These small plates of food are served to accompany and enhance alcohol such as ouzo, retsina, wines, raki and tsippouro. In fact, the Greeks have distilled alcohol as far back as the Byzantine era. Our infamous ouzo replaced the hallucinogenic causing 'absinthe' alcohol, which was popular in the 14th century. Meze can be served, hot, warm, or cold, and can sometimes comprise up to 50 small dishes. These can feature anything from a bread stick and olives to a platter of freshly-cropped herbs and salads, which we call 'horta' - 'Χόρτα'. They can also include kohlrabi, sliced and doused with lemon, and a satisfying piece of moussaka. In fact, meze options are often on a separate menu. You can also include any item from the a la carte menu to be included as part of your meze. Meze are not to be confused with appetisers, which are a meal course. Meze is a joyous occasion and celebration of life to be enjoyed in the moment, and as often as opportunity presents itself.

So going forward with this small introduction into the spirit of Greek cuisine, I have made a list of all dishes in this cookbook, which can be components of meze. You can add any amount of small dishes, such as olives, charcuterie, breads, salads, vegetables, and dips of your choice. Just do not forget your favourite tipple and finish with something sweet, or a selection of fresh fruit. You can also ask your guests to bring some meze dishes along with them. Just make a list, so that you do not duplicate the meze. Most importantly, do not forget to toast in Greek style «Στην υγεία μας « - to our health, which is hard to say without a smile on your face.

NB. Do not be overwhelmed at the prospect of preparing a meze. You can simplify any of your choices by scaling down the quantities of each recipe. For dishes, such as the frittata, you can choose one prized ingredient, such as mushrooms or asparagus. Once they are cooked in olive oil, you can scramble seasoned eggs into them. Bulk out your meze with shop-bought dips, breads, and olives. You could also schedule a meze get together for the day after you have leftovers from the larger recipes, such as the moussaka, dolmades, or pastichio. Then, you have a substantial starting point, from which to build 'kalin orexi' - 'Καλή Όρεξη'.

Translations

Glossary of English to Greek Translations

Please note that this is the Cypriot definition of translations, and that the Greek language is subject to many regional variations and dialect. I have also restricted the list to include words, which I have referenced in this book.

Good Appetite	Καλή Όρεξη
Welcome	Καλός ήρθατε
Sweets and Desserts	Γλυκά
Fruit	Φρούτα
Pasta	Ζυμαρικά
Orzo Pasta	Κριθαράκι
Seafood	Θαλλασινά
Meat and Poultry	Κρεατικά
Vegetables	Λαχανικά
Vegetable Stock	Ζωμός Λαχανικών
Vegetables cooked or garnished in oil (These are always suitable for vegans)	Λαδερά
Starters and Appetisers	Ορεκτικά
Legumes, Pulses and Beans	Όσπρια
Yellow Split Peas	Λούβανα
Chick Peas	Ρεβίθια
Lentils	Φακές
Cannellini Beans	Φασόλια
Broad Beans	Κουκιά
Wheat	Σιτάρι
Bulgur Wheat	Πουργόυρι η Πλιγούρι
Couscous	Κόυσκους
Rice	Ρύση
Potatoes	Πατάτες
Taro	Κολοκάσι
Artichokes	Αγκινάρες
Tomatoes	Ντομάτες
Celery	Σέλινο
Leeks	Πράσο
Carrot	Καρότο
Kohlrabi	Κουλόυμπρα

Cauliflower	Κουνουϖίδι
Onions	Κρεμμύδι
Spring Onion	Φρέσκο Κρεμμύδι
Garlic	Σκόρδο
Bread, Flatbreads, Filled Dough, Pastries - sweet or savoury	Ζύμες και Πίτες
Salads	Σαλάτες
Sauces	Σάλτσες
Soup	Σούϖες
Dips	Ντιϖ
Pickles	Ξυδάτα
Drinks and Alcoholic Beverages	Ρόφημα
Yiachni (A cooking method which stews meat, poultry, or vegetables in a tomato, olive oil and onion base.)	Γιαχνί
Kokkinisto (To marinade or cook in red wine)	Κοκκινιστό
Kathisto (To slow cook)	Καθιστό
Lemonato (To cook in lemon juice)	Λεμονάτο
Tiyanito	Fried
Vrasto	Boiled or Stewed
Fourno	Oven Baked or Roasted
Salt	Αλάτι
Pepper	Πιϖέρι
Lemon	Λεμόνι
Vinegar	Ξύδι
Oil	Λάδι
Groundnut Oil	Φυστίκι έλαιο
Vegetable Oil	Φυτικό έλαιο
Olive oil	Έλαιο Λάδι
Olives	Ελιές
Herbs	Βότανα
Spices	Μϖαχαρικά
Basil	Βασιλικός
Parsley	Μαϊντανός

Coriander	Κόλιαντρο
Mint	Δυόσμο
Dill	΄Ανυθο
Rosemary	Λασμαρί η Δεντρολίβανο
Thyme	Θυμάρι
Cumin	Κιμονό
Oregano	Ρίγανη
Paprika	Πάϖρικα
Bay Leaves	Φύλλα Δάφνης
Ground Cinnamon	Κανέλλα Τριμμένη
Whole Cinnamon	Κανέλλα
Whole Cloves	Γαρύφαλλο
Anise Seed	Σϖόρος Γλυκάνισου
Tomato Purée	Ντομάτα Πουρέ
Tinned Tomatoes	Ντομάτα Σάλτσα
Caper Berries (The edible flower buds of the caper bush plant, which is mostly consumed pickled and as a salad garnish)	Κουτρόυβι
Caper Stems and Leaves (The tender new stems of the caper bush plant, which are consumed in the same way as the caper berry)	Κάϖϖαρη
Cheese	Τυρί
Grated Cheese	Τρίμμα
Anari (A Cypriot whey cheese)	Αναρή
Halloumi	Χαλούμι
Feta Cheese	Φέτα
Yoghurt	Γιαούρτι
Milk	Γάλα
Evaporated/Condensed Milk	Γάλα Εβαϖορέ
Coconut Milk	Γάλα Καρύδας
Almond Milk	Γάλα Αμυγδάλου
Margarine	Μαργαρίνη
Bechamel Sauce	Μϖεσαμέλ
Egg	Αυγό
Cake	Κέικ

Filo Pastry	Φύλλο
Puff Pastry	Σφολιάτα
Sponge Cake	Παντεσπάνι
All Purpose Plain Flour	Αλεύρι για όλες τις χρήσεις
Self Raising Flour	Αλεύρι Φουσκώνει μόνη της
Semolina Flour	Αλεύρι Φαρίνα
Cornflour	Νισεστέ
Dough	Ζύμη
Bread	Ψωμί
Pancakes	Κρέπες
Kattimerka	Κατιμέρια
(Traditional Cypriot pancake)	
Sugar	Ζάχαρη
Honey	Μέλι
Chocolate	Σοκολάτα
Dark Chocolate	Μαύρη σοκολάτα
Rose Water	Ανθόνερο η Ρόδοσταμα
Rose Cordial	Τριαντάφυλλο Σιρόπι
Jelly	Ζελέ
Vanilla	Βανίλια
Nuts	Ξυροι Καρποί
Peanuts	Φυστίκια
Pistachios	Χαλεπιανά
Almonds	Αμύγδαλα
Walnuts	Καρύδια
Hazelnuts	Φουντούκια
Coconut	Ινδοκάρυδο
Wine	Κρασί
Meze	Μέσε
(A meal made up of many small dishes)	
Mesethes	Μεζέδες
(The component dishes of a meze meal)	
Vegetarian	Χορτοφάγος
Vegan	Νηστίσιμο

Veganism is a way of life - a spiritual state of being for a great number of Cypriots. This is particularly true for many periods of devotion during the ecclesiastical calendar. We refer to this practice as fasting - 'Νηστεία'. Food, which falls into this category, is called Vegan 'Νιστέμενο'.

Notes

Notes

Notes

Notes

Notes